NO FLUFF RENTAL PROPERTY INVESTING

Getting Started with Passive Income in Real Estate to Retire Early

---

DEREK SIMMONS

Contents

Part Four
Getting Started

Author's Mandatory Introduction

Do not skip it.
Read This First.

I am eager for the ideas in this book to work for you, for you to put them to work for you. For that reason, I have prepared a Property Walkthrough Due Diligence Worksheet and Offer Calculator for you. With it, you can hit the ground running.

One of the biggest difficulties with making a good offer is knowing how much money you'll have to spend on repairs. What makes it even more difficult is that you have to be able to estimate this on the spot. That's if you want to be an effective negotiator.

Imagine the scene. You drive up to a building and have 5 or 10 minutes to walk through it. Yes, you may do your due diligence and invite your professional inspectors, electrician, plumber, and all that once the building is under contract. You don't want to say to the owner you will go away to do your numbers and get back to him later.

No, you need to have the numbers at your fingertips.

The calculator is a one-page worksheet that you can use during your walkthrough. Print it and make notes or do the calculation there and then. It's pre-programmed for you.

To get your free calculator now, go to the link below (or scan the QR code). It may just be one of the keys to your success.

https://bit.ly/2yIdLPi

Got it?

Now let's get started.

Introduction

You think you want to get started investing in real estate, but have you no idea where to begin. You have heard that rental property investing can provide passive cash flow, and this sounds wonderful because you want to retire early or at least spend as few years as possible in a 9 to 5 job. You know there are other choices besides rental property investing, yet you are not sure what type is right for you, only that many consider rental property as the best option. But, you need the steps to finding, purchasing, managing, and well, the entire process of real estate investing. You have no experience, and while you heard you don't need any, you are at a loss as to how to start and be successful.

You sit at your desk, looking out of the window, wishing you could travel, spend more time with your family, or read a stack of books that have sat beside your favorite chair for 2 years. You know there are better ways to make money than by living paycheck to paycheck, working for 8 hours a day, 5 days a week. You want more besides a monotonous routine that makes you feel like your life is in a rut and always will be, and real estate investment could be the answer for you.

You have questions without answers.

- What are the types of real estate investment?
- Is rental property investing the best solution?
- What about REITs (real estate investment trusts)?

Building a rental property investment business not only provides financial stability but also freedom of location. You get to choose to work and gain self-fulfillment by providing accommodation to those who need it. There are not enough landlords in many places, willing to offer affordable housing, while also ensuring they make money out of their investment.

Benefits of Rental Investments

Only five benefits are listed, but as you learn more about real estate investing, you will find there are additional reasons to invest.

1. You own the property
2. You make money from the rent you charge
3. You decide who will rent the property
4. You can have multiple properties, in various states
5. You offer to house those who need it

Going through the pages, section by section, chapter by chapter, you will learn all the skills and knowledge required to succeed as a rental property investor. Not only will you learn how to structure your deal successfully, but you'll also learn how to find the perfect property, and most importantly, how to cultivate the correct mindset to persevere, and finally get your financial freedom.

It is easy to make mistakes, to misstep on your way to financial freedom through rental property investing, and that can make you wary of even starting. You are going to learn the way to combat these worries, to get over any psychological doubt that you can do this, and find the key to achieving your goals. No matter what you decide to invest your time in, you will only be as successful as you are willing to be, not only in the time you spend on the project but also in getting rid of your doubts. People who tell you rental property investments are dangerous or costly did not have a guide filled with actionable steps or if they did—these individuals did not listen—if you follow what is provided, you don't need to worry.

At the end of this book, you will be able to decide if rental property investing is what you want. You will have the keys to success, including how to apply the techniques you learn, the scripts and dialogues, systems, checklists, and marketing ideas that will ensure you succeed.

Inside these pages is a practical guide of actionable content which includes:

- The foundational knowledge to get you started
- How you apply the techniques shared
- What websites to visit
- Phone numbers and emails, you need
- Phone conversation techniques
- Templates for emails and direct mail

The content of this book is based on hours of research and years of experience in rental property investing. From rural Kansas to downtown Manhattan, I have invested in rental property, and so can you. I understand your hesitation. If there were an all-encompassing book or magic answers to real estate investment, we would all be rich. What I can do is use my experience, including mistakes, to help you discover actionable pathways to your own rental property investment plan, where you can earn financial rewards.

It is a book filled with information based on my

research and success to help you find your way into rental property investments. I have trained and led hundreds of prospective rental property investors in obtaining their financial freedom using the techniques outlined in this book.

I will make a promise to you—you can get started on your journey and gain enough knowledge to purchase your first property using the contents of this book. As long as you follow the information, soak it up, and do the steps, you will have the pathway to starting your rental property investment business, but your success depends on you, your mindset, and your willingness to work hard. No one became a million-aire by sitting around. They worked for what they wanted with the mentality of achieving their goals and the benefits their chosen profession offered.

Albert Einstein called compound interest the eighth wonder of the world. The compound interest of your investments and business ventures in years to come will be influenced massively by every little choice you make today. So, choose to proactively educate yourself and take the first steps toward ulti-mate financial freedom. The longer you wait, the less you will have in the future.

There has never been a better opportunity for you to start on your journey to financial freedom and early retirement than now. The internet and public records make it even easier to find rental property investments than it was 10 years ago. Much of the work and research is done for you and just waiting for you to take advantage of it. It is all up to you. Will you use the simple techniques and strategies outlined in this book to get the freedom you so desire and deserve? Or will you continue to grind out the 9 to 5, day in and day out? I have made my choice. Now it's up to you to make yours. I'll see you in chapter one.

Your Strong Foundation

SECTION ONE

You want to buy your first property today. The excitement is there, and you want the steps that will ensure success. Rushing into a purchase without the proper foundation and the steps found in later chapters often leads to failure. Just learning tactics is the wrong approach because you need to understand the whole market, how it works, and how it can change.

Let me ask you—do you build the roof of a house first or the foundation? Obviously, you need a foundation before you can put the roofing on your home. Without a proper foundation, everything falls down.

Establishing a good foundation will definitely improve your chances of success with rental property investments. As a new investor, you need to invest the time and effort necessary to master the underlying principles of real estate finance. More complicated financial transactions and analysis can require specialized knowledge, and this is not suitable for the most inexperienced investors.

In section one, you will learn:

- The mindset you need for financial freedom
- Tips on effectively changing your mindset
- How to run the numbers
- What it is like being a landlord

ONE

Pave Your Way to Financial Freedom

W hat is financial freedom to you? Each person has their perspective of being financially free, such as living a comfortable, modest life, with little travel versus wanting to have enough money to retire at 40. Before you can gain financial freedom, you need to create reliable, realistic goals.

You have bothered to find out if rental property investments are right for you; thus, you have at least one goal toward a better financial status. I made property investments successful because I enjoyed it, and I wanted to leave my 9 to 5 job for more freedom to do what I loved. I put in the work to build a proper foundation before I invested in my first property to ensure I was successful.

A good foundation leads to success, but it is not a guarantee. You need to have specialized knowledge of real estate topics before you can buy your first property, which leads you to create the mindset to reach your goals.

You have the controls to decide what property you are going to buy and the rental options you will offer. However, it all starts from a sturdy foundation and your goals because it is easy to make mistakes in real estate investments.

What Do You Want from Rental Property Investment?

Your path to financial freedom requires at least one overarching goal. Take a moment to decide what you want from rental property investments.

- Do you want the freedom to travel?
- Do you want to add more to your retirement account?
- Do you want to quit the 9 to 5 grind?
- Do you want financial freedom?
- Do you want to make life better for your children or need to support your aging parents?
- Perhaps you have been given a chance because of another's charity and wish to repay their kindness through your own donations or charitable endeavor?

You may not have a clearly defined goal, such as traveling the world while earning passive income, but you do know you want the financial means to make different choices.

Your purpose in investing should be direct regarding financial freedom; otherwise, the arduous work required will not seem worth it.

In any aspect of life, the mindset we have determines how successful we become. Your mindset may include financial freedom, passive income, and working less, but is that enough to keep you going when the first obstacle appears in your path?

Rental Property Mistakes

People without proper knowledge or time to set up their rental property investment business correctly make mistakes. Here are some of the most common mistakes.

- Hiring a property manager who doesn't do their job.
- Waiting too long to evict someone who is not paying rent.
- Buying a property that needs more maintenance than you can afford.
- Rushing into a rental because the price seemed right.

- Assuming it does not take time, knowledge, or a stable foundation.
- Investing based on "appreciation."
- Missing information in contracts.
- Carrying incorrect insurance.
- Buying too many properties.
- Buying without proper cash flow.
- Not keeping enough in reserve for maintenance and vacancies.
- Moving too quickly into the deal and missing inspection and appraisal reports.

You need a baseline of knowledge before you begin because not learning the steps leads to many of the mistakes above.

The Road to Financial Freedom

The six strategies below are the beginning steps to success for any endeavor you begin, not just rental property investment, but they definitely work for that goal.

1. **Focus on growth**. Treat your rental property investments like a business, not a hobby, or something to try to get rich. What risks are you willing to take on, what are your exit strategies per property, are you diversifying your portfolio enough,

what is your five-year plan? When you set your mind on the growth, you will make the proper strategic decisions to build your business quickly.

2. **Find your network's potential.** Who do you know? Who is available in the area that knows the market? You will want reliable developers, lawyers, contractors, and real estate agents. Buying rental properties is not your one-man-show. Right now, you are just beginning, so you may not have a network. You may need to learn how to build relationships and make new contacts to gain success and financial freedom.

3. **Look for efficiency**. What skills do you have and what skills do you need to outsource because you don't have the competence in the skills required? First-time and inexperienced investors struggle to conduct due diligence on their investments, which is why you need to know what you can handle and what you need to outsource for the most profit.

4. **Question any assumptions you make**. Always ask "what if" to challenge your thinking and overcome any biases you may have at the start. You have a guide, and sometimes the area you are looking to

7

invest in may not fit specific tactics, but with questioning assumptions, you can find a better way of doing things to work to your advantage.

5. **You need to have a plan and a purpose.** Do you plan on quitting your current job and focusing solely on rental property investment? Do you want it as a side business to help increase your retirement portfolio? Set up a strong plan, with the primary goal, and this will help you remain on the right roadway to financial freedom.

6. **Create the proper mindset**.

Mindset and Financial Freedom

You have an opportunity to gain financial freedom; however, you may need to change your mindset. We are taught from an early age that we must work hard, with a set schedule, and make money, saving plenty for retirement. The advent of the internet changed our perspectives a little by allowing more freedom in remote working environments and freelancing. Despite the changes, most of us consider a career to include 40 hours per week, at least, with a specific schedule.

Seminars and networking, including real estate courses, have helped us realize the potential for passive income streams. But these classes only provide you the foundation to start, your mindset determines if you will succeed.

Adapting your mindset is crucial. You need knowledge, determination, and motivation to build passive income streams, whether it is through rental property investments or other options. You already know there are common mistakes you could make, so how are you going to get beyond the difficulties? Will you give up at the first obstacle or find the motivation and determination to keep going? Let's look at a successful real estate investor and his beliefs about mindset.

Brian decided to invest in real estate. He invested in rental properties that are thousands of miles from his home in San Francisco. He wholeheartedly believes, just as I do, that mindset is imperative so you can push through the troubles when things do not go as planned. He earns a 29% annual return on his investments because he gained the correct mindset.

Investing in anything, whether it is a new appliance, or a piece of property requires thorough research. You are not going to bring a new appliance home without comparing brands, prices, and functions. You tend to look for the least expensive product that will do what you want because you want to save money. In real estate, what are the downfalls or benefits of finding the cheapest property? Can you gain enough profit or will your shopping habits end in failure? To avoid buyer's remorse, you need to approach the situation with a plan, including how to get around obstacles.

So, if you can develop the right mindset about rental property investing, then you could retire early, spend each year going on amazing trips, or buy that sports car you always wanted. You need to focus your mind and stop living paycheck to paycheck.

Focus on Mindset and Rental Property Returns

Let's take a moment to consider this guide to rental property investment. It is a guide designed to pave the way to your financial freedom, but what if you encounter an obstacle? I understand the herd mentality is strong. You want to keep following everyone else, working 9 to 5, and contributing to a 401k because it is comfortable, and although there are tough times, everyone is going along that path.

With your 401k, you are dependent on the stock market. If your chosen investment goes up, you get a bit of profit. But with rental property investment, there are five ways to help get a return on your investment.

1. Cash Flow
2. Appreciation
3. Tax Benefits
4. Rental Income
5. Inflation

You don't have the same parameters in your 401k that wait for other people to invest and increase the share price by increasing the demand. Let's consider different ways for you to earn passive income. You could decide to become a fulltime trader because of the flexibility and potential return on your investment. Stock investing is also about leverage, using more money to gain a higher profit. However, with stocks, if you lose, you have no way to recoup the money. In real estate, if you leverage to buy a home, you will have tax benefits, appreciation, rental income, and inflation working for you to help recoup the initial outlay of money.

So, what is the mindset you should have to use your motivation and determination to gain financial freedom?

1. Make sure rental property investment is a "burning desire." It should be the one thing you want to focus on, and the only thing you want to study.
2. Create a plan to achieve your goals; they must be realistic.
3. Act by creating daily goals that will take you a step closer to your financial freedom.

People who are prosperous and financially free follow the three steps above. They do not come home, turn on the TV, and watch endless hours of shows.

Instead, they look at their goal and what needs to happen before they go to bed for the night.

Warren Buffet is an excellent example of a savvy businessman. He has had a routine his entire life, which consists of reading numerous books and newspapers a day to choose his investment strategies. He believes you need to keep learning, even as you are taking action, and also, if you make a mistake, you get right back up and keep going.

Your goals will start with the desire to make rental property investing the only vehicle you use to get financial freedom.

Here is a list of some daily goals you might have:

1. Read another chapter of this book.
2. Look at additional resources and other books.
3. Contacting one real estate professional per week.
4. Examine the area you know best—the city you live in—for current real estate market information.
5. Study real estate ads to see what is available on the market.
6. Look through your current network and see who has their hand in real estate, construction, or mortgages.
7. Build your network, where it is lacking.

The list could go on. The essential factor—each day you need to accomplish a small goal—after you build your foundation and finish this book, you will be able to buy your first property or at least be closer to knowing what you need to do.

Sometimes the property market is stagnant, not allowing for a rental property investment purchase, so do not rush through the book or through your learning process and establish patience that the exact situation will appear when you are ready.

We have established that the proper mindset is imperative, so let's find out how to create an appropriate mindset for long-term success.

TWO

Mindset to Ensure Long-Term Success

B efore you can adapt your mindset, it would be helpful to know what qualities make a successful rental property investor. What skills do you need to have to start investing? There are several opinions on this matter; the list are skills professionals agree you need to have.

1. Time Management
2. Sales
3. Prospecting
4. Lead Follow Up
5. Presentation Skills
6. Qualifying Skills
7. Customer Relationships
8. Database Management
9. Consulting on Niche Issues, such as legal topics

Above are the nine skills you need to develop. Put yourself in the shoes of your prospective lender or partner. If you had a lot of money to invest, would you invest in yourself? You should become the type of person you, yourself, would invest in, and only then will others have confidence in you.

A successful rental property investor should make necessary sacrifices when starting out. You want to have an income higher than your expenses, by cutting down on the costs.

Real estate investors do not expect their goals to be as easy as opening a jar. A successful commercial or residential real estate business begins with buckling down, becoming frugal with your cash, and creating the most out of limited resources.

A vital attribute to have is grit. You must be able to succeed when setbacks occur and always, consistently, work toward your long-term goals to gain great rewards.

Knowing the skills you need is step one. Now we need to focus on the ten qualities you should have.

Ten Qualities of Real Estate Investors

1. You need to be comfortable with calculations. Financial managers make great property investors because they understand the principle between good

and bad debt. A person who can forecast cash flow and check the numbers before a decision is made will be more successful.

2. Social skills are paramount because you must be able to handle sellers, agents, lawyers, and vendors. You will need to negotiate the best deal for yourself while keeping good business relationships with partners, clients, and anyone else who will work with you.

3. Pragmatic people are phenomenally successful in real estate because they research, make decisions, and create realistic attitudes about potential success. You will require a flexible mindset, so you can handle hazards and complications that arise, and still earn a return on your investment.

4. You should be able to handle various matters, including the stress that can come from complications. You will need to manage the most critical aspects first while outsourcing or ignoring the smaller things.

5. Property investors who have goals, especially long-term, can achieve them by working with smaller goals first that help them reach their top target.

6. You should decide and move on, without wasting time on second thoughts.

7. Successful investors love learning about rental property investors, including current trends.

8. You should have the ability to work within a team, even if you are leading the investment, because you are going to outsource some of the work to those who know more about the niches, like the legal structure of deals.

9. Investors need to learn from others quickly. Others may have knowledge that will ensure your success. Don't get hung up on preconceived notions.

10. Effective communication is paramount to success. People who can listen, pay attention to details, and respond with professionalism are always going to reach their goals.

As you learn more about rental property investment, you will find information on learning the market and keeping up to date with trends. No successful investor goes into a deal without having as much information as possible.

Let's work on your mentality. When you bought this book, what was your goal? Now that you are reading about mindset, has that goal changed? If you are serious about financial freedom through rental property investment, then you should have some goals set to help you reach the ultimate investment goals.

The only way to keep your focus on the investment, whether you are looking at student, residential, or commercial rentals, is to have daily goals and a long-term goal of financial freedom. But within the overall real estate investment, you must also have a singular focus when you begin.

Who do you want to supply housing to? Use the three examples below as a guide to start thinking about your rental property investment goals.

- Students
- Single families
- Businesses

When you begin, your mind should be set on learning the steps to succeed, and how to keep your determination; therefore, a goal about the type of rental property you are going to buy is imperative.

Let's consider a small mountain town, near a national park, where hiking and camping is the focus. The city offers million-dollar homes, condos, and no downhill skiing. However, it also lacks affordable rentals. The two exceptionally low rent properties are always full. Middle-income properties are difficult to find because once rented, the tenants stay for years, even with small rental fee increases. A lot of the rental housing is available in winter, at most for 6 months of the year, where renters cannot have pets and must move out when the season takes hold. New builds are either for a specific client or to draw in more money from visitors who will use the housing for 3 months and close it up the rest of the year. No one is willing to invest in property and build more apartments, duplexes, or homes for the people who work in the shops, restaurants, and other industries. In fact, over half the employees working in the town live 30 minutes away in a larger city and commute. Several businesses have apartments they rent to European workers for 3 months during the height of the season.

Does the above situation sound like something you would want to help with? Building property to rent to those who genuinely need it, so they can live slightly better than paycheck to paycheck? Perhaps, your ultimate goal is making as much as possible, so you want to rent to the millionaires vacationing in some resort town?

Discover where you want to focus your learning regarding the market, so you can create the correct mindset for that goal.

Summing up the qualities, you want to remember there are risks, you have limitations, and your potential renter is the customer who is going to provide the funds for your financial freedom.

Steps for the Right Mindset

Successful rental property investors can bring back the calmness, even in struggles. You can learn to recognize when you are getting angry, anxious, stressed, needy, or scared about the investment you are entering into and help re-center your mind to deal with any issue that arises. Being able to remain calm and centered is imperative when you work with tenants, negotiate for properties, assess properties, deal with law enforcement, and other situations.

You do need to understand the bottom line, with regards to the potential return on investment and the issues that can come up like buying new appliances, repainting, or repairing something. You also have to have the mindset to walk away when a deal is terrible.

1. Think of mindset as an inner voice to talk to, and that challenges you. Your thoughts are telling you something, whether you are fixed in a current position and undermining your chance of success or if you are choosing to grow your mind.

2. Your inner voice can be detrimental, telling you to stop when there is a setback or challenge. Learning to interpret your emotions and separate them from rational thoughts is imperative to growing your mindset the correct way. You have abilities,

so how can you challenge those abilities without panic or upset.

3. It's all in your head, so feel free to talk back and work out a way to focus in a better manner.

4. Act once you have assessed, examined, and with a rational brain come up with a plan rather than reacting.

5. Also, think "yet," I have not learned that concept- yet. I will not buy a property-yet.

Our emotions and inner thoughts are often our downfalls to a decent mindset. We grow up focusing on the negatives in life, using the challenge of being told we "can't," or we failed to rise up and prove we can. Sometimes it backfires, and we instead become lazy and avoid the goals we genuinely wish to reach.

The mindset of people who reach their goals is one where they listen to the negative and turn it into a positive, by decluttering their emotions and looking at reality.

Let's consider a rental property situation. A married couple decided to rent out two homes. One was their main house, and the other was a fix and flip, they decided to keep as a rental. Their goal was to travel while making money from the rental properties to pay the mortgages. They left the management to a real estate agent, who did not pursue the rents, and by the time the two non-paying rental parties were evicted, the best course of action was the foreclosure on the homes. This couple made plenty of mistakes, and instead of thinking of rental property investment again, they are unwilling to allow themselves to get into a similar position again.

Are you the same way? Would you give up because you made too many mistakes, or would you try again?

The emotional reaction is to give up, but what if the couple learned from their mistakes, researched the market better, and managed the property instead of letting someone else do it?

- Think through your goal.
- Create a general outline, with new daily goals added each day.
- Act on at least one goal per day, whether it is to follow up a telephone call or research a new aspect of the market.
- When a challenge arises, think of your adverse reaction, breathe, and then write down at least three solutions.
- Choose the best of the solutions and act on them.

Psychologists and scientists tell us our brains are like supercomputers, offering us the ability to learn and change. You may have a mindset that gives up at the first stressor, but you can work on your habits.

One of the best solutions to get over any struggle is to use the psychologists' method for anxiety.

1. Write out the problem.
2. Describe your reaction.
3. List at least five things you would do differently.
4. Use one of the five in the list the next time a problem arises.

By following those four steps, you can help your mind adapt to a new routine. It works in just about any situation, whether it is related to anxiety or mindset.

Let's say you want to read another chapter of this book. Your obligations for the day have you working overtime. You are now working for 12 hours instead of eight. Furthermore, you will go home, find dinner, and then it will be late. Are you going to use the time to read another chapter or watch TV?

If your routine is to watch TV while you eat or in the evening to decompress from the day, you are more likely to decide to put off something else in favor of relaxing and feeling better. Hey, we all need personal days, but what do you want more?

Staying in the daily grind without financial freedom leads you to choose old patterns. Gaining more financial stability requires you to get over those habits and adopt new ones. So, using a routine, you typically fall into, write the problem, your usual behavior, and five ways you can change your habits. When the need arises, take out your list, look at what you want as a goal and find one of five ways to persevere beyond your habits.

Those who write about mindset have different perspectives on how it works. Some believe you can change a habit in 60 days, while others feel this puts too much pressure on you to succeed, and things end in failure.

Take a look at *Psycho-Cybernetics* by Maxwell Maltz and *Awaken the Giant Within* by Tony Robbins, both deal with more techniques for changing your mindset. There is no one "right" way to ensure your habits change. If there were, then we would need a few statements, and magically, you would be on track for rental property investing. Instead, we have *The Compound Effect* by Darren Hardy and *The Magic of Thinking Big* by David J. Schwartz to offer us more techniques beyond what you learn here and from the other two suggestions.

Each has a perspective on how you should approach mindset for the more abundant life projects, such as financial freedom, and how you can train your mind to gain your desires.

Your Personality

Your personality is going to matter when it comes to mindset. Who are you now? What traits describe you best?

- Are you a person with confidence in everything you do?
- Do you tend to be introverted versus extroverted?
- Are you tend to work harder when you have deadlines?
- Do you need someone looking over your shoulder to keep you on track?
- What stresses you out about current life obligations?

One of the best things you can do before starting rental property investment is to understand who you are now and who you need to become to reach your goal. A part of mindset is based on your confidence, skills, and determination. Plenty of people attempt to run a business or freelance work, only to discover they are better with someone standing behind them, ensuring they are keeping on track. Don't worry if you are a person who needs a boss because your network or potential partnerships are meant to complement the skills you lack.

I want you to make a list of your strengths and

weaknesses, including personality traits. After the list is complete, ask your family to review the list and add to what you wrote down. Discuss the points on the list. Part of this exercise is to help bolster your confidence, but also to help you see the reality of who you are, and the mindset changes you need to make.

The barebones truth—anyone can make a start toward their goals—few keep their determination and reach their goals.

THREE

Run the Numbers to Get Ahead

I s the rental property investment strategy right for you? What other investment strategies are there and why is real estate better? You could invest in the stock market (be it in individual companies, index funds, government bonds, REITs, or bitcoin). Investing in individual companies is riskier than buying government bonds, but cryptocurrency is the riskiest investment vehicle. You may be asking the question—how does rental property investing compare to these other options? One answer—property investing takes a lot longer than stocks or shares research, and there is a lack of liquidity with real estate investing. So, why do people invest in rental property?

Why You Should Invest in Real Estate

You can find attractive returns on your investment through multiple income streams when you put your money in real estate. Rental yield is a percentage of your direct rental income. Like any business, you have income and expenses. Your rental yield is the amount you receive for the rental fee less any expenses, which includes taxes and other costs to maintain the home.

Appreciation is another benefit of rental property investments. Homes, in general, appreciate in value. Value increases fluctuate, in the last ten years, some years showed a high of 8.9%, while the last two years were only around a 2% increase. When you decide to sell a property, chances are you can get more money than your original investment. You also have opportunities to get an equity line of credit against one property to purchase another to increase your rental yield.

Inflation can increase your rental income. Consider, 10 years ago, just after the housing boom turned into a crisis. Many people lost homes and had to rent. With waitlists at apartment buildings, more homes being rented than bought, it was possible to charge a higher rent than before the housing crisis. A one-bedroom apartment could rent for $645 before 2010, and after it was as much as $845. Now, most one-bedroom apartments are closer to $1,000. It does depend on the market one is looking to invest in, and some areas still have lower rents. The critical point—

you can charge more rent when inflation occurs, but any mortgage payment on a property is fixed. Your cash flow increases, while the cost of owning the property does not. Now, we do have more to discuss in later chapters about the downsides of investing, so while your mortgage remains the same, note that other expenses can fluctuate. Another aspect of inflation is mortgage rates. When mortgages are tougher to gain for people, like after the housing crisis, people turn to rentals, which increases the demand and lowers the supply, thus allowing the rental fees to escalate.

Many investment opportunities have "leverage," a way to increase your investment with putting a small sum down. Leverage allows you to buy more significant properties or more properties, rather than sticking with the amount of cash you have.

Paying down loans will free up investment resources, giving you access to equity.

You also have the option of improving your property to increase equity.

The above are just a few of the reasons why you should consider real estate investments. Now, let's take a look at the benefits of "income property."

Why Invest in Rental Property Over Other Real Estate?

Income property is property purchased to gain revenue. Any time you buy the property and rent it out, you own income property. The structure can be single-family, multi-family, or commercial. There are many advantages here including: you make the decisions, you have property appreciation, any money made is money in your pocket, your tenants are actually paying the mortgage, and you have tax write-offs.

Tax write-offs are definitely part of the calculation you make when deciding on which property to purchase. Current deductions include interest on your mortgage, interest on credit cards used to make purchases for the property, insurance, maintenance repairs, travel expenses, legal and professional fees, and property taxes. You also get to assess the depreciation of property. Note that taxes and deductions can change from year to year, so hiring an accountant is imperative to file your taxes correctly and with every possible deduction available to your business.

Real Estate Investment Types

There are at least seven ways you can make money owning real estate. Each one has its pros and cons. Before buying property, you want to understand the differences between these options to ensure you are making the right decision based on your cash flow and return on investment desires.

1. **Fix and Flips,** as Home and Garden TV (HGTV) has coined, it allows you to buy a property for less because it requires some small repairs to increase the value. You put funds into the home to buy it, to fix it up, and then resell it on the market for profit. It takes more knowledge or a good crew of people to look at a home and decide if it can gain profit from fixing small issues. Often, older homes have hidden costs you don't see because they are hidden behind the walls, or due to upgrades, an inspector may require. If you don't have solid education regarding home improvement, you may not have the time to take on the fixer-upper.

2. **Rent to own** is a long-term investment not designed to give you passive income. Under this option, you are living in the home, paying the rent, and as you pay rent, you are paying down the amount you owe to buy the house. At the end of the term, you must pay off the house. One way to do this would be to get a mortgage to cover the rest of what is owed. However, once you own the home and are paying

down on a mortgage, you are building equity, which does make a real estate investment.

3. **Buying vacation property** is another way, many people gain two things: a place to visit when they wish and rental income from renting it out through Vacation Rentals by Owner (VRBO) options. VRBO is the coined term to say you rent your home for a week, 2 weeks, or even a month or more to a person who is vacationing in the area just like you. You make money while it's rented but have a place to stay when you want to go out of town. Each state and city have rules regarding vacation property rentals; some have tight restrictions, where you must apply to have this type of rental, and depending on the number of applicants, you may or may not be able to rent it.

4. **Airbnb** is another popular investment option. Property owners can list a home on Airbnb and rent it out. You can rent a room or the entire house. Like VRBO options, you offer your property, but it can be your main home. You might decide for a week each month, you rent your home, gain a little income, and help pay your mortgage. Of course, with Airbnb and

your main home, you have to be okay with other people coming in and out, being around your home décor and belongings.

5. **You can purchase commercial property** and rent it out, just like you do with residential options.

6. **You can also buy your home, own it, and pay down the mortgage**, gaining equity as you pay off the loan, and the property value increases.

7. **Buying rental property** can mean renting out a room, apartment, half a duplex, or even several properties. The idea is to keep your expenses low, to keep the rent affordable, and thus keep your rental full of tenants. Successful landlords keep their tenants in mind and not just the money aspect.

As we get more into running the numbers, you will need to consider the different real estate options and the pros and cons. Key factors include value, risk tolerance, return on investment (ROI), the time you have, and the amount of control you want to have over the investment.

In 2017, a study conducted by the University of California-Davis, University of Bonn, and Deutsche Bank examined 16 countries and the rate of return on residential real estate. The conclusion was a 7%

return compared to less than 7% for stocks and 3% for bonds, per annum. Real estate allows for more ways to invest by purchasing the property that appreciates over time versus stocks that will increase as the supply and demand changes. Real estate can also provide cash flow monthly.

Real estate investment is more manageable for many people to understand versus stock investments because there are actual calculations a person can do to examine the return on their investment. You also have direct control over your investment, whereas stocks are controlled by the company, including growth, expenses, and other choices.

Bonds are another choice, and you can decide to work with corporate, government, or municipal bonds. The revenue earned is based on the maturity of the bond. A bond is designed to make money from interest, which allows it to be a minimal risk. However, interest rates do fluctuate. When comparing stock and other money market investments, bonds are more reliable; however, the profitability is meager, and your return is heavily impacted by inflation rates. When the interest is 3%, and the inflation rate is 1%, your return drops by one third. Real estate will gain during inflation because rents can increase. This is why rental property investment is one of the more profitable real estate options.

Real estate investing offers tax deductions, and stock investments do not. Bonds are not taxed on the federal level, which limits your deductions, and your income still has to be reported. Time frames can also determine whether you are willing to invest, and the type of income and capital gains taxes you wish to pay.

Certificates of deposit are a negligible risk option, with low-profit margins, when comparing to real estate. Interest rates impact certificates, so when rates are low, it is difficult to gain a high return, and you also have to report the income on your taxes.

REITs are a sound investment to get into the world of real estate, but there are definite differences. REITs can be anywhere in the world, and you share your investment with a conglomerate, whereas other real estate property options are full ownership by you, unless you decide to have a partner. A management company operates REITs, and several things affect your profits. REITs, according to Investopedia, provide annual dividends, around 2 or 3%, sometimes less. By owning property without other investors, you can have a higher dividend and more equity. REITs are also designed to be low yield with reduced risk in comparison to other investment vehicles. REITs are controlled by multiple parties versus expanding your investment portfolios on your own.

To finish out this part of our discussion, remember that stocks, bonds, CDs (certificates of deposit, issued by a bank, where you invest money for a set period), and similar investments depend on economics, market sentiment, and big investors. If you go against larger investors when buying a stock, you could lose everything. With real estate, you can weather the changes in the economy, as long as you manage your mortgage appropriately and keep your rents at an accommodating level for the current employment and economic situation.

Knowing the investment options, you can now think about what is right for you. Do you want to spend time learning the stock market, practicing with a paper money account, and then investing, hoping for a profitable trade? Those who choose real estate investments prefer less risk, knowing they will have a tangible asset that will eventually provide profit, whether it is from rent or fixing the home and selling it quickly.

Crunching the numbers is also about how much you have in the bank to begin your new endeavor. Before we look at what you should have to start, let's look at how much money can be made.

How Much Money Is Available to Earn?

Once we are done examining this section, you will understand home prices grew healthily in 2004 before the market bottomed out, and while home values are increasing in some states, others have not reached the same market value as before the credit crisis. As a homebuyer, you want to focus on specific locations and not the national trends because every state and city varies. Additionally, low mortgage rates indirectly affect home prices, where consumers are willing to buy when loans are less expensive.

The National Association of Realtors tracked real estate prices and offers median home prices from 1968 to 2004, where a 6.4% increase occurred, without a decline in a thirty-six-year period. In 1968, the median price was $20,100. By 1980, with an 11.9% annual increase, houses were costing $62,000 on average. Significant jumps such as double percentages stopped happening after the eighties; however, an average of 4% increases per annum occurred, with housing prices reaching a median of $185,200 in 2004. Prices increased about 1% up to 2006, and by 2007, the national average was falling at an alarming rate to the point that the median housing price was closer to the 2004 average and became stagnant. The market fell 30% in profitability, according to the S&P (Standard and Poor's).

Prices have increased, and so have the square footage options. In the 1950s, the average home was 983 square feet compared to 2,349 square feet in 2004. The homes increased in size, along with inflation adding to the costs of building, so of course house prices increased. Unfortunately, when looking at the national numbers, a boom in California with significant price increases can mask a downturn in a place like Detroit.

The reality is most real estate investments will not provide an overall profit in your bank account unless you sell the house. As you gain in value, your property taxes increase. Until you sell a home, the gains you see in value increases, are only on paper. Furthermore, tapping into your equity to expand your real estate investment can backfire as you suddenly used your home as an ATM without regaining the investment on the other property. There is every possibility of owing more on the house than what it is worth if you over-stretch your investment to keep expanding your real estate.

Mortgage rates are locked in for 30 years with a fixed interest rate, but when you go for equity loans or if you decide to get an arm with a balloon payment, you could end up paying a fluctuating rate with such massive changes that you can no longer afford the mortgage. Rates have been around 3.35% since 2013, and only in 2019 did they increase to 3.73%. Low rates ensure most people are looking to buy rather than rent.

The above might seem a little scary when you read your investment only pays off after you sell the property. You might consider the economy, various markets, and wonder if real estate is a bad investment overall. Actually, the calculation of profit is based more on an exit strategy to play the real estate game for maximum profit.

You need to understand the market sentiment

before you buy your first property. Are people willing to buy or rent? Are more people considering down-sizing to cut costs? Do more people need retirement communities? We will get back to these questions later.

To continue the concept of housing prices increasing in the US, yes, the prices are going up, and the pace is slow. The S&P showed the index increased by 3.13% in the second quarter of 2019, with 1.46% inflation adjusted. Prices increased by 2.29%. Nine-teen of the 20 cities examined, based on size, and ranking as major cities, showed increases, like Phoenix gaining 5.83%. Seattle declined by 1.32%.

The numbers are also based on regions; for exam-ple, in the mountain region, the highest house prices increased by 5.71% in the second quarter, whereas New England only gained 3.64%.

New home prices fell 1.6% to $388,000 as a median average in July, and the entire year showed prices fell 4.8% to $312,000 per annum. When exam-ining the housing boom, the crash, and recovery, most major cities are showing anywhere between -1.32 and 5.83% changes, where the recovery is mostly positive and around the numbers before the crash.

Residential construction is increasing based on new housing starts, completions, and permits, where there is a 6.6, 5, and 12% increase in 2019 from 2018, respectively. Foreclosures are falling, whereas, during the crisis, there were too many houses on the market to sell. For those with capital, it was a renters' market, begging for homes to be bought, fixed up a little, and rented to families in need. Now, it is harder to find an inexpensive deal because the mortgage mart is stable again, and people can afford to purchase a home.

Foreign investments are down, which is a good thing for domestic investors. Another concern is the changes in tax laws. For 2019, taxes changed, so ownership deductions decreased, taking some of the benefits away from investors that make real estate investments attractive.

The amount of money to be made is based more on real estate growth over a historical period, current market movements, and where you decide to invest. Yes, profit is about 7% per annum, but not all deals will be the same.

Examples of people who are succeeding in rental property investing will further help you understand the potential of this investment vehicle.

Claudia inherited a house in San Francisco. The house needed plenty of work because it was in poor condition. She and her husband decided to list the property at $1.3 million, while it was valued at $800,000. They received an offer for $1.45 million, all-cash, and closed in 10 days. Claudia and her husband were just trying to see if they would get a serious buyer.

Cynthia owned a home in the mountains of Colorado. Estimated worth, over a million, but the property is part of a land trust, so she was only able to sell for a little over a half million, after having the home on the market for over a year and a half.

The thing about these two stories is one was successful, and another was not. Claudia and her husband live in a city where people are buying homes, even in poor condition, because they are short on houses, and the views are where the value is. Cynthia is in a town without ski resorts, with beautiful views, but the land trust forbids touching any of the property, so any additions or changes to the house must come off the existing structure. No one could decide to sell a piece of the land for investment and allow a new build. Thus, the property is not really part of the investment, only the house.

Examining Claudia's final part of the story, they already had a home and jobs, with the earnings from the inherited house and projected life expectancy, a calculation of $20,000 per month in passive income results. But again, Claudia and her husband were lucky. They did not spend anything to get the house, and they were able to sell it without repairs, so 100% of the sale was profit.

Cynthia bought the land, built the house, and was unable to get as much out of the investment as she'd originally hoped because the market was different in her location.

Kim Bosler is another example of success. She invested in 13 properties and now has a passive income of $7,236 per month. Kim and her family live in California, and her concerns were gaining enough retirement income to stop working. Speaking with a financial advisor, she found investing in annuities and bonds was safe, but not going to provide retirement income. A friend suggested she consider real estate investing and helped mentor her, and also told her about the Real Wealth Network and Investor Academy that teaches some tips. Kim met with several people in her area who could help with her investments, including builders, lenders, and property managers. She and her husband continue to purchase property, earn off the rental income, and have a secure financial future.

Danielle and Wayne have 16 properties and make $8,700 per month. Not being experienced in real estate, they also joined a group to learn how to invest in rental property, networked, and have managed to gain without losing their cash flow.

Each time you see a story of success, you have to wonder, is it worthwhile to invest? Can I make money? The answer is—yes—with the right network, cash flow, and investment, you can make money. It all depends on where you are looking, the true amount of money is to be made based on the area and not on national numbers.

Key Calculations a Rental Property Investor Should Know

The money to be made in rental property investing varies and is subject to your knowledge of calculations. Running the numbers is imperative to ensure you understand the potential ROI. We will look at back-of-the-envelope, ROI, cash-on-cash, capitalization rate, Internal Rate of Return (IRR), and formulas that are necessary for choosing the right location and property.

Back-of-the-Envelop Analysis (BOE)

BOE analysis helps you discover if the potential deal is worth your time. If your BOE math looks right, then you can make an offer on a property, and let the inspections and other verifications occur. Warren Buffett said, in 2009, "If you need to use a computer or a calculator to make the calculation, you shouldn't buy it." He was referring to deals that should jump off the paper and tell you to act, rather than the method of overanalyzing until you are blue in the face. The numbers should be easy to see rather than something you have to play with to "make it work."

For BOE, you will look at income and equity, plus use income analysis tools including the gross rent multiplier, 1% rule, capitalization rate, 50% rule, net income, and cash-on-cash returns.

The income you make from a property is the money earned after you collect the rent and pay your expenses. Equity is what builds in the property as you pay off a mortgage, and it is what you would earn by selling the property.

Let's begin with the gross rent multiplier. It is the total purchase price divided by the yearly gross rent. If you buy a home at $144,000 and charge $12,000 for rent per annum, you will see a gross rent multiplier (GRM) of 12. If you buy a property at $300,000 and charge $15,000 per annum, the GRM is 20. A higher GRM means the investment is less attractive.

So, what does the GRM number mean? GRM is the number of years the property takes to pay for itself based on rental income. The GRM is helpful to assess properties with regards to depreciation, periodic costs, and costs you incur based on the renter.

Going back to the example, if you have a GRM of 12 versus 20, then you know in 12 years the property will start paying out to you in full rather than a GRM of 20, which takes eight more years to pay for itself.

The GRM is a good starting point, but not the only number to assess.

There is also the 1% rule, which examines the monthly gross rent. The rule states the gross rent of the property should equal at least 1% of the purchase price or better. So, if you have a property that will cost you $200,000 to purchase, including the repairs, holding costs, closing fees, and sale price, then you need to get at least $24,000 per year to meet the 1% rule.

Renting properties in high priced areas, with high price tag homes, rarely allow you to meet the 1% rule.

Once you have examined the GRM and 1% rule, you will want to move on to the capitalization rate. But before we get to that discussion, let's look at ROI and cash-on-cash concepts.

ROI

ROI determines the profit you can make from an investment. The formula is gain on an investment minus the cost of the investment divided by the cost of investment.

You pay $100,000 for a rental property. The closing costs were $1,000, and you had fix-up costs of $9,000. The investment was a total of $110,000. You plan on earning $1,000 per month in rent or $12,000 per year. You also have expenses such as the water bill, insurance, and property taxes, totaling $2,400 per year. Your annual return is $12,000 minus $2,400, which is $9,600. So, to find the ROI, you will divide the $9,600 (annual return) by the total investment amount of $110,000. The calculation is ROI= $9,600\$110,000. The result is 0.087, or 8.7%.

The ROI calculation is different when a mortgage is involved. You might need $20,000 for a down payment on $100,000. So, your closing costs would be higher upfront because of the lease. However, your total out-of-pocket expenses were less. You might have $31,500 out-of-pocket for the down payment, $2,500 in closing costs, and $9,000 in repairs. But you have a thirty-year loan, with a 4% interest rate.

When you plug in the interest, insurance, and other expenses, your annual return becomes less over 12 months. Your ROI is also based on the out-of-pocket amount, so the ROI percentage can be as high as 15.9%, depending on the expenses and rental income.

While the ROI percentage is higher, you also have to realize in the end; you actually pay out more over time. The yearly ROI is better because you put less in, but you are still paying the mortgage and interest rate, which increases the $100,000 to more than a cash-on-cash transaction.

Be careful when conducting ROI calculations that you understand all the principles and how it will apply to your actual earnings per year. The longer you have a mortgage outstanding, the more you pay in interest.

Cash-on-Cash Returns

We spoke about a cash deal above in ROI calculations, but you need more information to decide if this is the right way to invest. First, you have to have the amount of cash required to buy, and then you need to measure the annual return on the property to consider if it is worth it.

The cash-on-cash return calculation assesses the business plan for the rental property and the potential cash distributions for the lifetime of the investment. The difference between ROI and cash-on-cash return is the measurement made. ROI is about the total return, while cash-on-cash is only a measure of actual cash invested and the performance of the investment. You are going to learn the cash flow relative to the amount of money you spent before taxes when you do the cash-on-cash calculation and assess it for a current period (one year) versus the total time you intend on having the property. The calculation is one tool to help you estimate your potential earnings.

We will look at the purchase of a property that is a million. You put $100,000 down and borrowed $900,000. You also have closing fees, insurance, and maintenance costs of $10,000. For one year, you paid $25,000 to the loan, with only $5,000 going to the principle and the rest going to interest. What if you decide to sell the property after a year for $1.1 million? Using the cash-on-cash calculation, you would look at the cash outflow, which was $135,000, and the debt of $895,000. You are left with $205,000-$135,000 divided by $135,000 or 51.9%.

Another example is a property where you put in $1,200,000 with a $300,000 down payment. Your cash flow fewer expenses are $5,000 per month. Your income is, therefore, $5,000 before taxes for the month, and $60,000 per year. So, if you want the percentage of your cash-on-cash return for the net operating income, you divide $60,000 by $300,000 and see you get 20%.

The one thing about cash-on-cash return is the tax. You are not accounting for any taxes you need to pay on the income. Instead, you are looking at income before tax season. Each person has a different tax situation, with deductions and amounts owed. While you might see a 20% cash-on-cash return, it does not mean you won't send this to the Internal Revenue Service (IRS) at the end of the year. The formula also lacks any appreciation or depreciation issues that may arise, and risks associated with rent.

The takeaway—while higher levels of debt can drive up cash-on-cash returns, investors should carefully weigh the risks and be cautious about overextending themselves in a mortgage. You do not want to get so lost in the ROI and cash-on-cash returns that you forget the risks you might encounter, such as not getting all units rented and earning the "potential" income you calculated to consider buying the property.

Capitalization Rate

Capitalization rates are the industry standard for measuring property value. Otherwise known as the

Cap Rate, it is associated with the perceived risk and return a property has and it is measured as the ratio of the net operating income to the purchase price. Typically, it is expressed as a percentage. Properties with a high capitalization rate are excellent opportunities for small investors. However, you always need to do your due diligence.

The formula is capitalization rate equals net operating income divided by current market value. The NOI (net operating income) is the expected annual income. The NOI is determined from the rental income minuses the expenses paid out for maintaining the property. The current market value is the present-day valuation based on the current market.

When you are looking at a property for its worth as an investment, the purchase price you pay will be the current value of the property. The potential income or past rental income data will help you examine the capitalization rate. If someone can show you an estate worth $1 million and an NOI of $70,000, then your capitalization rate is 7%. The price is higher than other tools of investment, and therefore, a likely investment you want to make.

However, as you assess the capitalization rate and other percentages to determine if a property is worthwhile, you also need to evaluate the age of the home, location, status of the property, property type, tenants' solvency, terms of the lease, the market rate, factors that could change the valuation, and regional factors on a macroeconomic level that might impact your tenants.

The capitalization rate also needs to include an outlook on recovering your investment. A 10% Cap Rate means that it will take 10 years to recover your investment.

Internal Rate of Return

Another calculation is the internal rate of return or IRR. It helps you assess the profitability of your investment. The internal rate of return is a discount rate used to see the net present value of the cash flow on a project equal to zero. I know it sounds complicated, so let's look at the formula and calculation.

$$0 = P_0 + P_1/(1+IRR) + P_2/(1+IRR)_2 + P_3/(1+IRR)_3 + \ldots + P_n/(1+IRR)_n$$

where $P_1, P_2 \ldots P_n$ are equal to the net cash inflow in periods 1, 2 and n, respectively. P_0 is equal to the total initial investment cost, and IRR is the internal rate of return. You will decide how long you want to hold the investment before you do a calculation.

Once you have the time frame, you can begin plugging in the other values, including your initial investment, operation cash flow, sale profit, the return of capital, and the sum of those numbers. Most people use Excel to put the numbers in the calculation. Open a blank Excel spreadsheet and enter the numbers for the years you are assessing your investment. Then select create a formula and let the spreadsheet do the work for you.

Often the internal rate of return varies based on the size of your investment, rental income, and the cash flow you have after expenses. Some properties may offer 8% or up to 10%, but it also depends on the payments received. A rough year, with irregular fees, such as a unit standing empty, can affect the amount you earn.

You want to see an attractive IRR, but it does not need to be a substantial number. Sometimes bigger IRRs are not what you want to know because they can be misleading. You are looking for a metric that matches other calculations, such as cash-on-cash returns and equity. If the overall comparison of numbers from ROI, Cap Rate, and cash-on-cash returns plus the IRR indicate a savvy investment, you will want to continue assessing the property as a potential passive income maker.

There are a few more formulas you will want to learn to help you figure out whether a property is a worthwhile investment. Make sure you write these down in a place you can quickly grab them when you are working on property calculations.

- NOI = annual income-annual expenses (excluding debt service)

- Cash-on-Cash Return = annual cash flow / initial cash investment (expressed as a percentage)
- Payback Period = initial cash investment / annual cash flow
- Cap Rate = NOI / purchase price (expressed as a percentage)
- Purchase Price = NOI / Cap Rate
- Value-Added = incremental NOI / Cap Rate
- Debt Service Coverage Ratio = NOI / mortgage payments
- Loan to Value (LTV) = loan amount / appraised value (expressed as a percentage)

Getting Money to Pay for the Property

The calculations showed you how to assess potential investment earnings, now you need information on how to get money for your endeavor. You will start by using your own money. It is possible to use any savings you have to start your initial investment, but remember, cash flow is an imperative factor. You need to create a budget for real estate and personal expenses. If you use all your savings in a rental investment, with low cash flow or worse, no cash flow at all from the property and an emergency happens, you could be setting yourself up to fail.

Using Your Money

Setting a budget is the first step to figuring out if you can pay for the property with savings. A proper budget examines your revenue, expenses, and shows you your profit.

People who work for themselves are more likely to have an irregular income, which affects the overall budget. For example, a freelance contractor who chooses their projects will have a projection of the revenue required based on their monthly expenses. They must make a certain amount each month to cover their costs, and anything after that is profit. But what if there are no projects to take? What if some months end up with half the required income, while other months provide twice as much? The idea is to ensure that the slow months are covered by the busier months.

When you consider renting a property, you must account for the risk of one or more units remaining empty.

Let's say you have $100,000 in the bank, and you find a property for $80,000 that you want to buy. The calculations look great, and there is a current renter in the property. What you don't know is the renter is in an unhappy marriage. Suddenly, the couple divorce, and your unit is empty. You try to find a new renter, but no one wants to pay the price when upgrades are needed. Now, you need to spend your other $20,000 to make repairs, but you cannot increase the rent because the area will not support it. All the rent will be additional revenue on top of your monthly income, but it will be a slow process to recoup the $100,000 in savings. Suddenly, your home requires a new water heater, but you have not regained the savings yet, and the rent is not coming in because you are not finished with repairs.

The example could go on, but the point is simple; you want to budget using practical information, keeping in mind the potential pitfalls that can occur.

Using an accounting software program, or an Excel spreadsheet, fill in a budget form. Enter any mortgage, car loans, insurances, and other expenses you have for your personal life. Fill out another form for the rental property projections, including current rent and costs.

Using the budget forms, assess your main home and the investment property for potential repairs. Water heaters used to be lifetime appliances, but now most last for 10 years before they need to be replaced. The same can be said for most home appliances. When was your roof on both houses done? What repairs have been made, and how often have you made repairs, plus the repairs on the rental property that may need to be done.

What is your emergency budget? According to financial experts, you need at least 2 years of income in the bank in the event of a significant health issue or job loss. You have monthly details for how much you currently spend; however, you need to plan for things that might arise when considering how your current income works. When adding in the rental property income, you need to allow for expenses for that home, plus any points when the property might be empty. If you use your entire savings or need to dip into it for those times the property is not rented just to pay the mortgage, you are setting yourself up for a tricky situation.

Here is a list of things to consider when creating a budget for personal and rental income.

1. Use online tax tools to project taxes paid for the year. Many of the tax calculators available through H&R Block, Credit Karma, and other tax sites help you calculate your monthly income and your potential yearly tax amount. Successful rental property investors put 40% of their income into a tax account. Others take 25%. You want to consider where you fit in the tax bracket, and make sure you are putting that much aside each month.

2. Cash flow is imperative, so when you are getting money, you need to save as much as possible, not spend it on things you do not need.

3. Prepare for the cycles that happen, such as

increased heating costs in winter or more expenses on air conditioning in summer.

4. Have separate accounts for your business expenses, personal expenses, and savings. There are many reasons to have more than one account, the IRS likes a clear distinction between business and personal. It also helps you keep your income streams separate. By using savings accounts for tax money, you can be earning interest.

5. Plan to save the first 5 years of your rental income. Expenses come out of the income, and you want to save the rest for taxes and potential costs that might come up. In fact, depending on the GRM number, you may want to hold out until you have reached that number before you start taking profit from your investment. If it was 12 years, then hold back spending the income you make to help cover periods of trouble, such as not having rent coming in.

These suggestions help you figure out whether you want to use your money for the investment or if you want to get a loan. You never want to put yourself in a position where you have a negative cash flow from your current job because you are covering for your passive income investment.

Bank Loans

If you are going to get a bank loan, you need to have a good credit rating. We discussed calculations for when you have a bank loan versus when you use your money, so while you budget your personal and rental business, consider what you need when it comes to potential vacant homes and how you will cover the mortgage for the rental property. You can quickly go from an excellent credit rating to a poor one when you make mistakes with bank loans.

You can check your credit rating for free in many ways, but the top two websites are creditkarma.com and Experian.com. You can also visit usa.gov/credit reports. Three other sites which you may find useful are moneysavingsexpert.com, credit.com, and credit-sesame.com. Plenty of credit cards have started offering at least one credit agency score, such as Discover offering Transunion.

You should understand the websites that offer a credit score for free from Transunion, Equifax, and Experian, but these numbers are not your Fair Issac Corporation (FICO) score. Your FICO score is often something you need to pay for or have run by a bank to see if you are investment worthy. FICO is based on the Fair Isaac Corporation, and most lenders use this score for mortgages. Your score can be between 300 and 850, ranked from poor up to exceptional. A poor score is below 579, the fair is 580 up to 669, Good is

670 to 739, Very Good is 740 to 799, and anything above 800 is exceptional. Your scores are based on payment history, debt, and length of credit history, new credit, and credit mix.

Your Vantage Score, which is shown by the three major consumer credit bureaus use payment history, age and type, percentage of limit used, total balances and debt, recent credit behavior, inquiries, and available credit. The scores are still ranked similarly, but you will notice the three major credit bureaus can be slightly different in scores even when using the same information to rank you.

Starting with a good credit rating is important, but you should access your FICO score at least once before you begin your search for property. Most websites will require a payment for the score, which is another reason you need to know there are two different scores, Vantage Score and FICO.

The best loan rates are available for those with exceptional credit, but as long as you are in the high "good" range (700-739), with a FICO score, you can determine if you can get a fair rate of return on your investment or if the loan interest rate will take too much of your profit.

Improving your credit rating requires you to assess your credit history. Payment history accounts for 35% of your FICO score. Anyone with a discharged bankruptcy skipped or missed payments will have a lower rating. Those who make payments on time each month will have a higher number. However, if your amount owed exceeds your income, your score can lower. The amounts owed or debt to income ratio is 30% of the score. The length of your credit history accounts for 15%, and new credit is 10%. The diverse types of credit you have accounted for makes up the last 10%. You can have the best repayment history and low debt but have a lower score because your past is short, you have no new credit, or your credit mix is lacking. You should show a payment history for a car loan, credit cards, and mortgage to have a decent credit mix.

Student loans do not count. Lately, you can request your credit agency to start looking at your utility bills as a way to have a broader credit mix.

If your score is on the lower side, it is possible to improve it using the following steps.

1. Check what is reported on your credit report. Get rid of inaccurate information and errors. You can do this by accessing your credit report through Credit Karma and Experian and filling out a request for removal.
2. Remove any discrepancies (such as an address incorrectly assigned to you).
3. Ask for anything over 7 years to be removed if it is detrimental to your score, such as a credit card with missed or past

due payments. Only closed accounts can be deleted, and this is important with anything negatively affecting your score, even if it shows a long credit history. Remember, the length an account is open is only 15% versus 35% of steady payments.

4. If you went through a bankruptcy, you must wait for 10 years before it falls off your scores. Otherwise, it will affect your scores.

5. Pay down any account, such as revolving credit (credit cards) that have over half your limit used. You want to show low debt to income ratio, but also ensure that your accounts are less than 50% used. Otherwise, it reads as "high" debt.

6. Pay your bills on time.

7. Use your utility bills to improve your score. Credit Karma has an opt-in choice to access your utility bill information and give you credit for payments you make.

8. Only open new accounts when needed.

9. Don't close unused credit cards, unless the history reflects poorly on your account.

10. Do not make too many hard inquires as they can impact your score, and too many over an extended period will lower your amount. If you want a mortgage, have a

company run the FICO score and then
take the result around to other companies.

Depending on the troubles you have with your credit score, if any, it can take 2 to 10 years to improve your score. The quicker you pay down your debts and keep making payments on time, the faster you will see a score improvement.

If you need to build more credit because you have a thin file, start with a secured credit card, after a little while, open another credit card, and in 3 to 6 months request a credit limit increase if the card company doesn't already provide one. The point is not to use these credit cards, but to have the accounts and build a history. You can use the card once a month and set it up to be paid off immediately, automatically. This shows you are making on time payments and keeping your debt low.

Ensure you are paying installment loans, like auto, mortgage, and student loans. Pay these on time. You can also consider a secured loan like a CD loan, where you borrow against an amount you have for collateral.

Any company that reports to a credit bureau has a cycle of reporting every 3 months, although this has started to change with people wanting to improve their credit scores faster and the internet. Lenders have an easier time to update scores quicker than in decades past automatically.

Make sure you have revolving credit, charge cards, service credit (utilities), and installment credit to round out your credit history. In as little as a year, if you pay off loans, reduce credit card debt, and make payments on time, you can see a twelve-point bump in your Vantage Score. Sometimes you see at most 8 points increase due to the 3-month reporting term; however, because not all companies report in the same month, you could see a change of two points per month for 12 months. It just depends on how diligently you work on your credit scores. It takes a long time to get to 800 if you are coming from bad scores, but remember, many banks will work with you if your score is in the good (679 to 739) range.

There is a fine line between improving your score by paying off as much debt as possible and keeping money in a savings account. The ultimate goal is to have your debts under 50% for revolving credit and pay on time to your installment loans while keeping your entire debt below the 50% mark for your income. Always show you make more than you spend.

FOUR

What's It Like Being a Landlord/ Property Investor?

Being a landlord can be great because you earn passive income, but there are times when the stress of managing a property can become overwhelming. We are going to look at a "day in the life of" and a "month in the life of" a rental property landlord.

The responsibilities you have as a landlord can vary, depending on how much work you will do. Do you have construction experience or property management knowledge? You may need to hire a property manager and contractors for some of the rental tasks. Daily life can include contacting these professionals to check on their work or to schedule repairs.

You will receive rent once per month. Most require the payment on the first of the month, with leeway until the third. However, depending on when the mortgage payment is due or when the lease was signed, the rental amount might be a different day. Rent owed on the first helps you keep track of the fees due. If a person moves in with half a month left, you can prorate the rent for the first half of the month, with another payment due on the first or set up a deal to include the first full month plus the prorated amount.

What responsibilities you have regarding the utilities will be up to you. Is it a multiple unit property with only one electric and water meter? If so, the landlord pays for the utilities, but often increases the rent to accommodate those fees. Some people have trustworthy renters where the services can be combined. For example, one property has five houses on the land, where individual water meters finally got installed, but the main meter runs through one particular house. The water bill goes to that tenant and is part of the individual electric bill. The tenant pays the whole bill. However, the propane for heat is based on two tanks for the five houses. One tank goes for two homes and the other for three. You would calculate the usage based on individual meters and divide the cost for the propane and water. For the tenant with the water bill, the landlord subtracts the four properties water usage from the propane bill. Or requires more money or reimburses the tenant for the portion of the water bill paid that was not part of their usage.

You want to set up a situation where you have a

favorable income with minimal time spent on expenses. Apartment complexes typically charge a rental fee, break the water fee down based on how many people are living in the apartment, and charge a small garbage fee. The electric, internet, phone, and TV are usually the tenant's responsibility. However, it all comes down to the calculations you do and whether you find savings in providing expenses as part of the rental fee.

The first or last day of the month is best for rent collection. Unless a payment is delayed without your knowledge, you may visit the collection box each day until all payments are made. With online banking, many landlords have also provided other methods of payment, including bank transfers and PayPal.

Most of your daily work as a landlord is conducted passively, once you have a property and unless you are looking for new investment. Most landlords want more than one property to gain more passive income. Once you have established the first property, you are most likely going to start researching a new investment, which requires daily phone calls, emails, and real estate searches.

Monthly Items

Anything can happen when you own a house. Pipes breaking, minor repairs, major repairs, and problem tenants can affect your daily life as a landlord by filling up your month. When a home is in good repair, you might think about some of the monthly things that need to happen.

- Change Heating Ventilation and Air Conditioning (HVAC) filters (once a month, 3 months, 6 months, or each year)
- Winterize the home (cover external pipes)
- Snow removal
- Rental collection
- Handling tenant calls for small leaks, running toilets, appliance issues
- Light bulbs (should be tenant obligations, but might fall to you for hard to reach or change fixtures)

Some months are going to be just as passive as daily life as a property owner; however, some are not. You could go a few years being a landlord without having any issues, and then suddenly pipes are breaking, significant repairs are required, or redecorating is needed because a tenant moved out.

There are times when variance and title issues may appear that were not caught during pre-purchase inspections of the contract of sale. You might take a few months, some attorney's fees, and eventually get things worked out.

Problem Tenants

There are degrees of problems that might occur with your tenants, such as a late payment that becomes a few late payments, and then a missed payment. The tenant may have trouble with a "moving paydate" such as a holiday or weekend interfering with their direct deposit. Most landlords require an additional fee for late payments, and you may have to chase those funds. However, problem tenants can be a real headache when they do not pay or attempt to make up missed payments in the next month. There are legal proceedings you must follow when you have problem tenants.

Each state will vary for the specific process; however, you are going to need probable cause to seek an eviction. It must start as soon as things become troubling. Record everything.

Before a tenant moves in, you want to take pictures of the home's condition. You must log any call the tenant made and your response to that call, whether it was for a minor repair or something more substantial.

Your lease also needs to be as transparent and inclusive as possible, regarding rent, noise, pets, and other terms. If other tenants complain about a tenant, record those conversations, including the time, date, and the discussion.

Consult an attorney at the beginning. Do not wait

until you think you have sufficient evidence to proceed with an eviction. Bring the first issue to the lawyer and let that person tell you how to proceed.

When it involves missed rent for the first-time, you need to wait until your grace period is over, then send a letter or email. You can also make a phone call, but you need a way to track your communication, so a letter or email is imperative to show date, time, and reason for the request.

If the rent does not get paid, you can send a letter requesting the tenant move out or pay. You will need to be kind, but firm. Do not let the tenant say they will pay you double the next month. Require partial payment or full payment. The idea is not to threaten eviction with the first rent letter. Only after you've asked three times for total rent to be paid without any response or partial payment will you be able to evict. Late, but full payments are not subject to eviction. It can make your month stressful; however, as long as total rent plus any late fee is provided, you cannot pursue the matter in court.

Problem tenants are also the reason you never want to overextend yourself when it comes to cash flow. The repairs, court fees, and missing rent can all lead to trouble if a tenant does not pay or worse wrecks your rental before moving out.

There are horror stories you should be aware of when it comes to problem tenants. Some landlords have had kitchen cabinets, all appliances, toilets, and any fixtures removed from a house by an unhappy tenant. They take these things and sell them. You end up replacing everything. People have also gone so far as to remove pipes, put a hole in every wall and tear up the carpet or flooring.

You can take the tenant to court, but the reality is you may never see the money for the damages or missed rent. Often problem tenants are savvy regarding the law enough to hide their money, mainly based on how the lease is signed. If only one person living in the home signs the contract, you can only name that party. For example, a married couple might have only the husband sign, so only he is liable, and then they can hide any money they have under the wife's name.

Make sure you always have every person's name on the lease who is 18 or older. You want all tenants to be responsible for damages and not just one person.

FIVE

The Timing of Success

You want passive income now. You want instant success. But life is based on reality, and the time frame to gain success as a rental property investor will vary based on your goals. The more money you want to make in a month, the longer it will take for you to reach that goal.

When to Expect Success

It is honestly not going to come in a matter of days or weeks, but it doesn't have to take a decade either.

What is your income goal? Do you want a thousand more a month, or do you want ten thousand? What is your current financial status? Do you have at least a hundred thousand you can invest, or are you starting with twenty thousand to ensure you have an emergency fund?

Each person's situation is different from their credit scores to their savings. It is also about when you can find the right deal.

Remember our example of Claudia, who inherited a house and sold it quickly? She is an example of what could happen but rarely does. Things are often more like Cynthia. Cynthia put her home on the market in May of 2018. She rented to own from August until she could evict the people living in the place. She never saw a dime of rent, and the people renting the home glued the oven door shut. It sat empty for an entire year, and instead of the $1.4 million it was listed at, it sold for just over $500,000.

Never be impatient for success. Take your time and outline a business plan with realistic aims.

How Much Time Will You Spend Working Per Week?

We all have lives. Things can interfere with our goals. You may have a forty-hour workweek, and suddenly your boss needs you working 60 hours. The amount of time you have to spend on your rental property endeavor determines when success will come. However, if you are willing to lose a little sleep to continue your learning phase and research potential properties, you will see progress much earlier than someone who keeps putting off the work.

Buying your first property, you are apt to spend

just as much time as after you have a few properties purchased, should you continue looking for new investments.

For those who are happy to have a couple of properties for the moment, you will eventually spend less time working on property buying and more time ensuring the rents are coming in and enjoying daily life as a landlord.

There is no right answer about how many hours you should spend per week on your rental property investment business. Some days you will be going around for 12 hours and others you won't have anything to do at all.

For example, while you are learning the current market by assessing locations and potential properties, you have plenty to research. Once you have a property in mind, you'll wait for the bank and the inspections. You may also have over a week to wait and see if someone will accept your offer. Yet, you are not going to sit around while you wait to see if the deal will go through. Instead, you should be looking at runner up properties. If the first falls through, is there something else you want to invest in?

The key—the amount of time you spend may or may not change depending on your goals, but the types of tasks you complete are modified based on the stage you are in at the moment. You should not stretch yourself too thin when creating a routine for rental property investing and success.

- Set a reasonable goal.
- Outline your business plan.
- Figure out the amount of time you can invest based on other work and family obligations.
- Begin with a daily task until you reach success.

Success is subjective; therefore, you determine what your success will look like and work toward your investment goal.

Finding Your Goldilocks Property

Now the foundation is laid. You are ready to find the right property so you can gain financial freedom. You will learn how to get started in rental property investing with actionable steps. We are going to delve deeper into property classes and property types. In the end, you will have all of the information regarding location, the types of properties that make the best rentals, and how to make deals.

You already know the mindset you need and the financial basics, and if you skipped the first chapters, then make sure you go back and read them first. A solid foundation is necessary if you want to succeed in rental property investment.

SIX

How Do You Get Started in Rental Property Investing

F inancial information and mindset prepare you to get into the first deal of rental property, but what are the actual steps to rental property investing? Getting started is about your commitment to the project and building wealth using real estate. For most people, buying one property that offers one to four units is a safe and effortless way to get started. Traditional methods of real estate investment start with a realtor, who will take your specific needs and walk you through securing a bank loan through one of the major institutions like Bank of America, and help you finalize the purchase. It is a straightforward, well-documented process, and unfortunately, doesn't make the greatest deal. Two central problems exist with this method.

1. You probably don't have a handle on what a "good deal" is yet.
2. Your realtor is not going to take the time to find the perfect rental.

To get around the first problem, I recommend you find a real estate mentor, someone you can talk to one-on-one who will share their experience with you and help guide you through your first deal. Mentoring relationships are a function of human culture, whether you are being mentored for a plumbing business or real estate. If you have not been a part of a mentor-mentee relationship, take the time to read up on it and figure out the most successful programs. Real estate mentors may charge you a fee for their knowledge to increase their passive income; therefore, research is imperative to finding the correct person to help you. A mentor should be someone willing to partner with you and help guide you without fees. They should be prepared to have you work for them and with them for 3 years, at least, in the area you wish to form your rental property business. Three years helps you establish your goals, set a foundation, and build more income toward your first rental property investment.

Your mentor should be someone who is in the same property industry as you, for example, if you are going to fix-up a property and then rent it, you want someone who can teach you those steps versus a multiple-property landlord who builds and then rents.

Creating the mentor-mentee relationship, you do not want to challenge the knowledge the person is passing on to you. Do not question them but place yourself below them socially. If something does not sound correct or you read something that contradicts the expert, form your question with kindness and request clarity. Challenging the mentor's position can end the relationship, create distrust, or make it harder for you to learn.

For example, "I can't ignore that bill, it will go on my credit," is a challenge statement. You could instead ask, "What will affect my credit, and what is the advantage of doing what you suggest?" In this way, you are asking for clarity, without challenging them and showing a willingness to learn. You do not have to follow each step your mentor teaches you. If something feels wrong, you can take their advice and then make your own decision. Most mentors join you because they see potential in you as part of their social network. Be open to gaining wisdom and learning from their life experiences.

The programs that require you to pay for the mentor's time are often ways for the person to make income. Some mentors go in with the idea of helping and seeing where you can be of value to them, but others are looking for a passive income stream and do not wish to share their secrets. For this reason, you should do your due diligence on which mentor programs are best and see if you can find someone willing to help you go around and learn without a fee associated with it. Mentors can also frame a deal of making anywhere from 1% to 20% of your first deal from the rental income for a specific period as payment for helping you.

Steps to Find a Mentor

1. Speak with real estate agents in your area
2. Go to landlord association meetings
3. Research programs found online or through seminars
4. Communicate with potential mentors to get a feel for their knowledge and if you can work well together

When it comes to the second issue, a realtor is not as motivated as you to find a great deal. The lower the price of the property, the less the realtor makes on the commission. A realtor wants to make a good deal, not a risky one, and will not want to low-ball the seller. You are also going to find most realtors pressure you into a close, whether you are done with the due diligence or not. Realtors are also trained to show you at most 4 properties that fit your criteria and then tell you to "Put up or shut up."

You can visit properties without a realtor being involved. If it is on the market, you can swing by to take a look at the outside, grab more listing information from the flyers, and research the area before you ever utilize a realtor. You should look at hundreds of listings and visit at least a dozen properties before you make a purchase. Remember, an unsatisfactory first purchase can set your goals back years, so you need to be prepared mentally to do the work and then approach a realtor.

There are several ways for you to find properties without a realtor being involved. Craigslist, local papers, online websites, and local landlord meetings are just a few. Many neighborhoods have landlord organizations that meet monthly or bi-monthly. Attending these meetings can help you find the right contacts to conduct your business. Landlords can also have real estate for sale, and you may find a mentor among the group.

Check out websites like National REIA and Sharplaunch.com to learn about landlord associations in your area.

Real Estate Licenses

Since commissions, supply, and customers motivate realtors, you may decide the better option is to get your real estate license. A real estate license allows you to sell a property without paying commissions to others, so you obtain 3% of the value of your purchase in cash or as a discount on the property. There are fees to get the license, and it takes time, but the amount you save is worth it. For example, a $250k property allows you to keep or make $7500 back because you are the realtor on the deal. The license portion of becoming a real estate agent is around $1,000 in most states.

The benefits of getting your license include accessing the Multiple Listing Service (MLS) database, adding to your income streams, networking, credibility, and gaining more tools and resources unlicensed professionals do not have.

As a realtor, MLS is imperative to information regarding homes for sale. Typically, you will have a fee each year to keep accessing the MLS, and you will want to become a part of the National Association of Realtors. The association helps you connect with professionals in your investment areas. You also need to spend around 30 hours in class to get the license and maintain it.

You will want to be careful with regards to liability as a licensed agent. You should make upfront deals. Full disclosure is essential when buying and selling real estate. Your title as a realtor can lead to complaints and litigation if you go through underhanded means. The seller, if unaware you are cutting the price down for yourself, can come back to sue you.

Before you decide to become a real estate agent,

make sure you know the laws, the procedures you must follow, and what happens when you are investing in rental properties and representing yourself in the deal. The fees you save on the deals are definitely beneficial; however, not every investor finds it is worthwhile to become an agent. They are happy to utilize the benefits of a licensed agent without going through the turmoil of classes, paying for a license, and keeping up to date.

SEVEN

An Overview of Property Classes

P roperties have specific classes they fall into, which is helpful to know, so you start your investment correctly and avoid competing against those who have more cash flow. Small investors are better off choosing a market segment that avoids direct competition with larger investors. Larger, more conservative investors tend to gravitate to Class A properties, creating high demand and lowering returns. Class C properties and secondary markets can sometimes offer overlooked and attractive opportunities for smaller investors.

Class A Property

A Class A property is built within the last 10 years or includes historical homes (fully renovated). These properties don't need refurbishment and tend to have fewer maintenance issues. The idea is to buy the properties and hold them for investment. Most buildings have the latest in modern amenities and high-end finishes like hardwood floors, granite countertops, and stainless-steel appliances. Class A properties have a higher price tag and provide a lower cash flow. For people with limited funds, there is a rather significant downside to buying one of these properties.

The only sure way of making money is to have a higher rent, but you also have to consider if the area can handle it. Most of the homes are found outside of major cities or in owner-occupied communities. The good thing about the homes is how well maintained the properties around your rental would be. They also tend to be areas that can support a high income, have good school districts, infrastructure, and shopping centers. The neighborhoods also have low crime rates and decent medical facilities. Vacancy rates are low, and there is a higher demand for investment properties, making them easier to sell and gain a profit.

Class A properties are considered a low-risk asset due to the security the rental property investor has with them, including lower expenses and fewer maintenance problems.

The only downside for you starting out is whether you have the initial investment and a potential renter to ensure you can keep the property.

Class B Property

Class B are slightly older, often 10 to 30 years in age. They tend to be lower quality but in good condition, in decent neighborhoods, and are remarkably similar to Class A choices. More maintenance is the biggest issue with Class B properties. The cost of buying a Class B is less than Class A, and you tend to get a better capitalization rate from Class B. The properties are a bit riskier to purchase and lease, but typically the investor-owned properties are rented out without trouble.

Class B properties will have a lower-income tenant, and the rental income will need to be less than a Class A. A nice benefit is desirability and the growth potential of the property. With a small investment, you can eventually upgrade the property to a Class A. You also have a high potential for steady cash flow.

The benefits are definitely something that should keep your interest; however, do not forget that too much put into the investment to make it a Class A property, and you could be doing yourself a disservice. There is a fine line between having renters and putting too much into a property so that you make the units or home unaffordable for those in the area.

For example, let's say you upgrade the property to a Class A, but you cannot convince any Class A renters to move into the area. Are you able to charge a Class A price with the Class B renter? Chances are the renter is going to look for similar rent to what they were paying before the improvements because it is what the budget allows for rather than an increase of $50 or more to their current lease.

Class C Property

Class C properties are over 30 years old, and they are not renovated. Typically, they have deterioration and outdated systems for electrical and plumbing. You will need to make repairs and be on hand for maintenance issues. The properties are usually found in less desirable, lower-income locations with a higher crime rate. Rental rates are also low. People have low-wage jobs or pay rent with government subsidies. Properties are also mostly investor-owned rather than owner-occupied.

The lower acquisition costs make the investment of Class C properties desirable. You do have a potential for high cash flow, and with the correct strategy, you can have a very profitable venture. But the risks you carry are much higher. You will need to make improvements as you can and sometimes immediately after the purchase of the property. Furthermore, the condition of the property can affect your financing options, where some loans are just not available to you.

Class C properties are a better second or third property, if not something you look for a few years down the line, when you have more experience. You need to be experienced in both real estate investment and as a property manager to ensure you keep the property fully rented.

Class D Property

Class D investments are older buildings, like Class C, and often in a more deteriorated state. You will need to make numerous repairs before you can rent the property. You may find a bank is willing to help you make the purchase, but the insurance may not want to cover anything until you make updates.

An example of this is a property in a small mountain town, with five houses on one piece of land. The original owner built it in 1920 and owned it without a mortgage. As the property owner grew older and could not maintain all the properties, they also let the insurance fall away. When an investor bought the properties, numerous repairs had to be made before the buildings could be rented, let alone before the insurance company would fully cover the homes. Due to the mortgage on the property, the new owners had only a few months to get the homes livable and covered by insurance before the mortgage company would decide to pull the plug due to "no insurance."

The property was in a town with rental needs, but most Class D properties are in low rent neighborhoods where crime and drug abuse are high. Finding reliable tenants in such areas is extremely hard because the tenants have low income, bad or no credit, and those who are decent, law-abiding citizens are scared of those around them.

You are going to see the lowest acquisition costs with Class D properties. You should also see a high price to rent ratio, where you gain the right amount from your investment, but you must understand the local market thoroughly. You may also discover the Class D is better as a fix and flip, where you rent it for a short time after it is fixed and until you can sell it at a profit for what you initially invested and the fix-up costs.

Class Ds should be avoided if you are new to rental property investing.

Summing Up Property Classes and How to Identify the Classes

Your ability to invest in a property will determine whether you should look for Class A, B, C, or D. However, as a newbie to the investment market, you want to stick with Class B options that are more affordable and in need of few repairs. The rental income may be smaller than the C or D, but you are also not required to spend as much time each month on the property. Unless you have a large bank account, Class A is a pool that is difficult to break into as your first property.

Now that you understand the property classes, we need to examine how to identify them in a search. Several websites can help like MLS or Reonomy. You can pull up listings in the location you want to buy a property. It can be generalized, such as state-based or citywide. The idea is to do a broad search, so you do not miss anything worthy of your investment money.

You will need to add an asset type filter to search for a property type, such as multi-family or duplex. Bear in mind, you do not want to be too specific in the search parameters that you miss something utterly worth buying. Obviously, if you do not want to invest in a new build, you want to get rid of new homes or land searches. Consider if you're going to narrow your search for units, lot sizes, and square footage.

The year built, and the price are two other ways to identify properties by classes. Remember anything built in the last 10 years will qualify as a Class A, so if you are interested in Class B, you need to set parameters for older homes in good repair.

As you look at the properties for sale, make sure you assess the sales history. How many times was the property sold? Is there a reason for the frequency of transactions? Is the property currently listed at value or below value to the comparisons nearby? Once you have identified potential properties, you can visit them. For Class B properties, you will want to look at multiple neighborhoods that are up and coming, have a low crime rate, and have a mid-range level of income.

EIGHT

Property Types for Rental Property Investing

An overview of property types has been mentioned to help you with other rental property investments, but now we should examine residential, commercial, and retail investment potentials and then examine each type of housing.

Residential, Commercial and Retail

Residential property investments are those you lease to single families, whether you have a multi-unit or a single-family home. You are not able to rent these properties to a person who wants to run a business out of their home, such as a doctor's office. Commercial investments include retail and office space. The property is designed to house a type of business, preferably one that is going to be around for a long time. Retail space can be challenging to invest in based on area. You might notice retail locations that always have turnover because the market just doesn't support what goes into the buildings. In some instances, with retail, it is about economics, and other times it has to do with newer space being built in a nearby area. Office space can be in a strip mall or a larger building; it just depends on the amount you have to invest.

Under each of the main property types, we have further classifications to discuss.

Condos

Condos are usually in a structure of 3 to 4 units, much like apartments. Apartments can be 3 to 4 units, or over a hundred. Still, for somebody starting out, a smaller complex is more affordable and more often for sale without being a part of a REIT or property management company.

Condos are similar to townhomes. Condos are usually part of a larger property, like an apartment complex or office structure with office space on the lower floors and living spaces above. Condos are connected by hallways, where there are communal spaces such as pools, game areas, and more to keep the owner of a unit entertained.

Townhomes are individual houses that share one, two, or three walls with another townhome. They are adjacent homes with community areas, although some may not offer a playground or pool. Homeowners Association (HOA) fees for condos are generally higher because a property management company sees to the outside of the units, while each person in the condo keeps up the interior of their space, only. Townhomes require maintenance from both the HOA and the owner. The owner maintains the indoor space and any individually fenced outdoor area, but the HOA is responsible for painting the exterior, replacing exterior fixtures like the roof, and maintaining communal grounds, including the road into the townhome area.

Townhomes tend to be in urban areas, whereas condos are in the city. With a townhome, you usually have a little land that goes with the property, and with a condo, the interior is yours. Safety is higher in a condo because of security officers, and the privacy is less due to sharing a floor and multiple units on the floor with others. Townhomes are single or two-floor homes with a single car garage.

Condos and townhomes can be pre-sold. When new units go up, there are usually advertisements to tell people there are places to buy. However, because they are new, the price is generally competitive and higher than buying an older condo unit. These units are not a bad investment for the right price. If you can make the rental income you require to pay the HOA fees in full and the mortgage you have on the property, then you might want to consider one or more units. However, condos typically do not rent for enough to cover your expenses.

Furthermore, the HOA fees are higher, and regulations may not allow for investment. You cannot expand the property, and you are limited by the condo regulations. Some regulations do not allow you to be an owner-investor and rent the property.

Townhomes are different. As an individual unit within a 2 or 3 building setup, the HOA cannot regulate you as much. You can rent the property as long as the tenants are keeping to the HOA rules. You can get enough in the rent to cover the HOA fees and a mortgage, of course, this depends on the initial investment and the area.

Single-Family Homes

Single-family homes come in many forms, from ranch style to tri-level locations. You can find homes in the city and outside of it. When you consider investing in a single-family home, you are looking for one renter. You want this renter to remain in the house for as long as possible or to have a vast pool of people that will rent it immediately if it becomes empty.

An excellent place to consider looking for single-family homes is in an up and coming area or near a college campus because people are moving in and out of the city all the time. Near military bases are also a good idea since some families want to live off base but know they cannot buy a home without having to sell it in a year or three when their position requires a move to a different state.

As an initial investment, you want to go with a Class B, and on the low side, so you can eventually use the rental income and additional savings to buy another single-family unit.

The size of the home should compare to the current market trends, but also fit within the mid-line. For example, downsizing has been extremely popular as well as tiny houses, but you may find in 2 or 3 years, five-bedroom homes are desirable again.

Multi-family Real Estate

Multi-family units include an entire townhouse building, duplex, apartments, and single-family homes with apartments above garages or mother-in-law units that you can rent to more than one family. Multi-family homes are a good starting point for those who want to rent one half of a duplex or make a small amount of income from an apartment off their garage or home. If you need to make an investment where you live in part or most of the house, to start your rental property business, you can do so and prove to the mortgage company that you have supplemental income to support a better mortgage.

You want to consider all aspects of multi-family

homes from multiple apartment units to a single unit attached to your main house.

REOs and Foreclosures

A Real Estate Owned (REO) property is typically foreclosed by the banks. Foreclosures are marketed through the usual means, although in some instances, you may find these homes go to auction, where a bank attempts to get the best price possible. Some banks sell packages of properties to hedge funds or banks, specializing in real estate. Most of the foreclosures will require fixing them up, but you may be able to rent them during this time. Contacting a bank will help you get in touch with REO deals, and you may find it is the best market for you to be in; however, I have not seen an investment bear enough passive income to tempt me. The deals available depend on the area, your requirements, and the occasion. Some people only look for REO and foreclosures as part of a rental and fix and flip.

Fixer-Uppers

Fixing up a property is often about reselling it versus the long-term investment. However, to gain a better rental fee, you may consider looking for deals that allow for rental property investment with a decent income. Fix and flips tend to be low on the value scale and require you to be careful in the amount of work you project and fund. Too much of an investment may put you in the negative for earning income. If possible, you can rent these properties while you do some of the fixes, but that can also be tenuous as the renter may not want you entering the property to make the changes.

NINE

Location, Location, Location

You have heard the chapter title phrase before whether you've been interested in real estate or not. Location is always the key to any investment, whether it is your home or a rental. You have a choice to buy locally or try your hand at remote investments. There are advantages and disadvantages to both approaches, which you need to understand before you move forward.

Buying local can provide you with a competitive advantage over other investors, particularly those who will be absentee landlords. The average person already has a wealth of knowledge about their community, which can be beneficial to invest in the correct properties. You also have intimate knowledge of the market and close proximity to the rental, which can help you overcome any disadvantage you might face in a less than attractive marketplace. Of course, there are numerous reasons you might be compelled to invest in a remote market, and you will need to take extraordinary efforts to mitigate the disadvantages of not being local.

Why Location is Important

If you watch any of the HGTV shows or go to a seminar about real estate, the first thing you ask is why location is imperative to buying property. The place has to do with value and property type. You already learned there are certain property types easier for you to invest in and with better returns on your investment. As you assess the location, you also ask if the home is a worthwhile investment or if you are just throwing money at it.

Location is about the purchase price, value, and your intentions. Value is assessed based on the purpose of the property. The main home is something that can increase in value over your life, whereas a rental property might need to gain value quicker so you can enjoy the equity. Value for an investor is based on income production and ROI.

We discussed fixer-uppers in our property type chapter, you will remember, you want to put as little into the investment as possible while increasing the value. Flippers or speculators wish for a quick profit, so they look at an undervalued property that will be bought and sold at a better value.

Location determines value, whether something is undervalued, and will remain that way for a long time or will gain it quickly with a few updates. Land is not something you can move, obviously, but you could pick up a house from its foundation and set it somewhere else, at significant expense—the point—location sets the value. Topographically speaking, higher-valued homes tend to be in the city center. Those who cannot afford the city center must commute at least 30 minutes, if not closer to an hour, just to have a place they can afford. As new, small shopping communities develop and more neighborhoods and schools increase, the values of homes also increase, despite the long commute.

Denver and the area around Denver International Airport (DIA) is an example of how communities can begin at a lower value and explode with development. When the airport moved from Stapleton to become larger and handle more air traffic, there was nothing around it. After almost 30 years, DIA is now like a city of its own, with numerous neighborhoods. Housing costs went from around $100,000 up to $150,000 to more than $350,000. The new builds are closer to $400,000 and half a million. The older homes are being bought, flipped, and then sold at similar prices.

The families who could afford to live there, if they bought their homes, are still able to survive and work around the airport and in many of the new stores and hotels. However, those who rented are having to look at places in lower rent neighborhoods, closer to the old Colfax area, which tends to have gangs and crime. The apartment complexes are pushing out the low to middle-income families due to the competitive rental costs.

As people move away from the city centers and new shopping centers that make mini villages, the prices continue to lower, but there is also the cost of commute that has to account for the expenses one pays.

Assessing the location and value is imperative to choosing the right property for your intentions as the investor and must rely on economic changes.

Price to Rent Ratio

Calculations and formulas are something you are always going to use, and it applies as much to the location talk as our previous discussion on money to be made from rental property investments.

The price to rent ratio equals average property price divided by average annual rent, which is equal to the average property price divided by the average monthly rent times 12.

Let's say the average property price in Los Angeles is $812,571, and the average monthly rent is $3,324. The price to rent ratio for Los Angeles would be $812,571/ ($3,324 x 12). The result is 20 for the cost to rent ratio. But what does this mean for you? A low price to rent ratio is between zero and 15. Average ratios are 16 to 20, with high being anything over 21.

The rent is a comparison between whether it is a property to buy or rent. A lower ratio shows the prices are low compared to the average rent you can receive, versus a high price to rent rate, where the property sells for more than you can probably rent it. A moderate number can show it is an okay rental, or it may be too high and is better for a long-term purchase investment. An average market makes it hard to tell what should happen. However, most experts, including me, believe you would be able to rent the property more than someone would be willing to buy it.

You do not want to use this metric as the only deciding factor about location. You do want to use it to determine the average rent, and whether you could gain that much in the area you are considering buying.

You can find as much information as you need to complete the calculation based on the city you are researching. Mashvisor is one website, but there are a dozen that tell you where to get city-data regarding the US housing market. You also have the opportunity to find investment property calculators, neighborhood pages, and information to help with the average property price and rental income amount.

What are the Best Websites to Research Location?

You want to use websites that will provide the data you need with trusted sources. The top three include neighborhooddiscount.com, realtor.com, and nar.realtor. However, if you want to know about population size and demographics, unemployment rate, household income, housing prices, interest rates, or daily traffic counts, refer to the data sources below.

- Population size and demographics - US Census Bureau (census.gov)
- Unemployment rate - Bureau of Labor Statistics (bls.gov)
- Household income - Bureau of Labor Statistics (bls.gov) & US Census Bureau (bls.gov)
- Housing prices - FRED economic research; HUD (fred.stlouisfed.org) (hud.gov)
- Interest rates - FRED economic research (fred.stlouisfed.org)
- Daily traffic counts - Data.gov
- Public schools - Data.gov
- Building permits - Data.gov & Local city offices
- Commercial real estate sales - Costar (costar.com) & LoopNet (loopnet.com)

The list above provides the type of data you require and notice you may have to view more than one website to find all the information you want. For example, daily traffic counts, public schools, and building permits can be found at data.gov, whereas, demographics are accessible by the government's census website.

TEN

Which Properties Make the Best Rentals?

W e've discussed property types by classes, which has more to do with value and purchase price than what makes a great rental. The criteria below will help you narrow down your risk and seek a better investment. The suggestions are based on your desire to have long-term rentals without a substantial risk of vacancy. However, if you have opted to rent in a college market, some of the things below may change.

Bedrooms

One and two-bedroom houses tend to have a high rate of turnover for renters because a single person will meet the guy or girl they wish to be with and suddenly want a second bedroom, then they start having kids and 3 or 4 bedrooms are necessary. Long-term rentals to families keep your vacancy expenses down and rent coming in, so you want at least three-bedroom houses. Also, they sell better when you are ready to move into your next investment.

For multi-family structures, two-bedroom apartments or duplexes are acceptable and common to find. Single bedroom apartments and studios are also shared, but you should expect more turnover with smaller apartments and a waiting list for two or more bedrooms.

You don't want to go up to five bedrooms or more unless you are in a college or university area. Having more bedrooms is not always better, even if you are trying to attract a family. Yes, you might get a steady renter who has five kids, but often the property costs become excessive. The truth is kids can be hard on homes, where you need to repaint, fix broken windows, replace the carpet, or other issues.

Age of the Home

Who isn't attracted to an older home with character? Investors understand the repercussions. An older property will be less expensive, in most areas. However, the cost of fixing it up will soon take away any of the potential income you were hoping to make. Older homes are not as energy-efficient, utility bills are higher, this limits your tenant pool. If they are responsible for the utilities, then they are going to look for something that will be on the lower end of the cost scale. If you roll the utilities into the rent, they will still know the rent is higher because of the expenses you are attempting to cover.

This does not mean gems don't exist. If you have the budget, the time, and can make the rent you need work, then sometimes a deal doesn't need to account for the age of the home as much as other features.

Garage

Where do you live, and what area are you attempting to invest in? Single-family housing with a garage is more often the appealing choice because the tenant wants to store at least one car inside, and they want to store boxes and other belongings. For example, if you invest in a home where you want to attract a family with kids, you want to provide a garage for the renter. The kids will want to store their bikes inside. Living in snow or heavily wet areas also require a carport to make the tenant more comfortable. Long-term tenants tend to stay longer if there is a garage as part of the deal.

Utilities

There is a fine line between paying the utilities and making the tenant pay them. A savvy renter will do the math as they look at properties. What are the features of the rental? Are utilities included? What is the rent compared to properties with similar amenities with services included or not included?

Your job is to ensure you understand your market share and provide a comparable rent whether or not you pay the utilities. Older properties are something you tend to pay the utilities on to hide the actual costs, but it is not ideal for you. The trouble is when a tenant is not responsible for the utilities, they tend to be lackadaisical about windows, air conditioning, and more. They might leave a door or window open during winter, unconcerned about the heating bill. Instead of using windows and doors to cool things down in summer, they may run the air conditioner twenty-four seven. Worse, if they do not pay for the water, then you may discover a higher bill because of a faucet dripping, multiple showers in a day, and much more.

You want to find a property where the tenant covers all utilities such as water, garbage, sewer, electricity, and heat. If necessary, find a property you can have a master metered system, where you can see what each tenant uses and divide the costs appropriately.

Lawns

Who wouldn't want a little outdoor space to relax and enjoy? Some tenants are never going to use the outdoor space, but they are exceedingly rare. Most people enjoy having friends over, cooking on a barbecue, and enjoying a little lawn. To gain a long-term tenant, you want to maximize the outdoor space, whether it is a community option or a private lawn or yard to keep the tenant happy. Attracting families definitely requires outdoor space.

Parking

Providing one parking space in a tight location is better than having no parking, but ideally, you want to offer at least two places for your renters to park. If you can provide three or more, then that is even better.

Nearby Amenities

To attract renters, you need nearby amenities, such as a safe place to jog take the kids to the park or get groceries. People also want to send their kids to a good school and have a minimal commute to work.

The most suitable types of investment property for small investors tend to be existing multi-family dwellings like apartments or mobile home parks, multitenant rentals, offices, and even self-storage facilities. Since you are just starting out, you will want a 3 to 4-unit building, so if a single vacancy occurs, you are only losing 25 to 33% of your gross income instead of 100%.

Foreclosures are often an excellent place to start looking because you can do some repairs and find affordable deals. Foreclosures happen because people could not afford the mortgage they had or took out too many loans against the property. Sometimes they are in disrepair due to angry owners leaving, and other times you can find a gem.

You don't want to look at buying land and building a home. Most construction costs are over $125 per square feet, which equates to a three or four-bedroom home around $400,000. When you add in the price of land being extraordinarily high or difficult to build on, you want to stay away from the higher initial investment, not to mention the time it takes for a build. Most builds take 6 months with a full crew and pleasant weather for completion and the Certificate of Occupancy for allowing people to live in it. Imagine putting in $100,000 with a construction loan of $350,000 and not being able to recoup your costs for at least half a year if not a full year. Vacant land and building are not suitable for the first-time investor.

ELEVEN

Analyzing Deals

E arlier, you learned various formulas to analyze the metrics of a property. Now, you have been assessing potential deals in the ideal location, and it is time to consider some other tools and notes.

Online tools help create a rental property analysis report. You can find the zilculator online as one example. When you use this tool, it offers an executive summary, including the location, type of property, how many units or bedrooms, the year it was built, and the investment strategy it should have.

You can then look at the purchase price, average monthly rent, cash flow, and cash-on-cash return. All calculations, including the cash-on-cash return, IRR, Cap Rate, GRM, debt coverage ratio, operating expense ratio, after repair value, and profit/equity from rehab details, are provided. The report from this site will also provide a financial breakdown based on the purchase price, costs, and repair costs. It also offers the operating analysis broken down so you can learn the NOI and potential tax liability. Sales history and comparative market analysis to see what else is happening in the area will help you analyze the deal in more detail. For example, as you analyze transactions, are there other rentals in the area, what do they rent for, how long, and what are the similar attributes?

Zilculator is just one online tool. You also have balancesmb and financialsamurai as high-level overview websites allowing you to analyze the property before you buy it.

Remember, the three most important points for your calculations will always be the adjusted income, which is the gross scheduled income minus 10%. You also want to look at the adjusted expenses and see if you are gaining at least a 45/55% split in your favor. Lastly, recalculate the fair market value. The current income and actual expenses information used to help you find the NOI for valuation is helpful.

Additionally, prioritize projects where you find value-add opportunities, but you also need to resist overpaying for the unrealized potential a property has. Look for properties with a robust and diversified cash flow that ensures ample income, so for your debt service ratio (principal plus interest payments), you want a low ratio because it means your portfolio is healthier. By doing this, you will have the cash flow you can reinvest into a new property and also have a margin of safety should a unit stand empty.

Is Cash Flow More Important or Is Appreciation?

Your investment style and the neighborhood you invest in will tell you if cash flow or appreciation is more important. Some areas are neglected, which means appreciation is stagnant. Most investors, including myself, prefer to make money rather than lose it in hopes that a sale in the future will bring in an attractive investment. I tend to invest in cash flow rather than appreciation. If I can buy a property with a positive cash flow at the end of the deal, it means I have found a good deal. Should appreciation occur along the way, all the better.

The other way to look at cash flow is if you put a large amount of money down to buy the property, you are going to have equity in the home, which equals cash flow. Appreciation is great for neighborhoods that historically show a steady rate of appreciation. You want to try for 25% down on any property to increase your initial equity in the home. Equity can be used for cash flow later.

What Does It Cost to Run an Apartment?

The expenses of running an apartment vary from state to state due to energy and other utility costs. For example, in Michigan, the electricity is sent in from a neighboring state, so there is a fee a person pays to get the power from the other state, plus the usage fee. People in Michigan pay double for their electricity, whereas in Colorado, the costs are straightforward, and heat is produced in-state, so they have lower bills.

You will want to look at the important costs:

- Payments, Interest, Taxes, and Insurance (PITI)
- Water/Sewer/Trash
- Utilities
- Maintenance of the apartment
- Maintenance of the grounds

The cost analysis usually shows $50 per month, per apartment not including the services and PITI, so if you gain a loan of $100k, you should expect to pay $1000 per month on it and then you have your taxes that can vary wildly based on the type of property.

Run the numbers once you have an area you wish to invest in and a building that looks ideal.

TWELVE

Finding Your First and Subsequent Deals

You are ready for your first deal, but you still feel you need some practical steps to get started. Once you pick a geographic target market and determine the type of property you want to invest in, the goal shifts to identifying specific properties for potential acquisition. To do this, you need to cast a wide net. You also want to make sure you are bookmarking loopnet.com and MLS sites like realtor.com to keep referring back to when you are searching for your first and subsequent deals.

The MLS

MLS is short for Multiple Listing Service. On the MLS platform, you can find property for sale by different brokers around the US. When you access realtor.com or redfin.com, you are looking at the updated MLS list.

The Newspaper

Quickly fading from our world are newspapers, but for some of those golden deals, it is where you want to look. Newspapers have for-sale-by-owner property listings the MLS may not show.

Word of Mouth

Despite it being old fashioned, word of mouth is still a useful concept. By telling people you know that you are in the market for rentals, you can build your network and find some deals. Maybe a neighbor is looking to sell, and they need a certain amount from the deal, so they are willing to work with you to avoid the realtor fees.

Craigslist

Craigslist, like any online platform, has had its difficulties. People have been scammed using the site, but due diligence can save you from some of the most embarrassing issues. Individuals turning to Craigslist want to save money by running a classified ad for free. Even renters use the site to post their openings.

Outbound Marketing

Using advertisements, direct mail, and other marketing techniques, you can bring sellers to you. Combine this with a real estate license, and you can find some of your first deals with ease.

Loopnet.com

Another online marketplace, this one is for commercial properties. You can also find multi-family apartment complexes, shopping malls, and fast-food restaurants on the site.

To use these tools to your advantage, you want to cast a wide net, yet set up as much automation as possible with alerts for you to review. When emails come in from realtor.com or other websites, you can look at the properties, screen them based on your criteria, and then visit only a few of them. Your initial alerts should use qualitative property screening, where you confirm the property fits most or all of your criteria for location, type, condition, and class. A virtual survey can help you figure out if the home is worth your time, but if there are few pictures or no virtual 3D tour, setting up an on-site survey might be worth your time.

Buying Your First Property

SECTION THREE

Once you have found your property, you will need to buy it. But what goes into making the purchase? You want to look at purchase methods, coming up with the down payment, tips for working with banks, and finally executing your first deal.

THIRTEEN

Purchase Methods to Consider

There are many approaches to financing your first deal, and you want to consider all of them before you walk into a real estate office. There are pros and cons to each investment strategy.

Property Investment Strategies

There are half a dozen strategies to use and learn about.

Raising Money from Others

One way to purchase a property is by increasing the money from others. The advantage is gaining access to higher cash flow. You also partner with knowledge-able people who can help leverage and compound the income to optimize your real estate deal. Extraordinary growth potential lies in working with others, and you must understand the potential returns that offer better appreciation for your cash flow. A partner requires you to share control and profits. You also need to have significant trust in your partner(s) to make sure the deal will be successful. The advantages far outweigh the disadvantages, especially knowing you can compound the leverage to make a higher profit.

Counterparties can be family, friends, or private investors. Before you consider working with family or friends, there is a caution to be made. When money is involved, not all family or friends can be relied on, but then again, with a private investor, you have to make sure the legal partnership has no loopholes, and the person is legitimate.

Lease-to-Own Approach

Find a homeowner in mortgage trouble, such as a home that is near foreclosure. Enter into a lease-to-own deal where you will buy the property. Then, you are going to have a person in the house that rents the property and their rent goes to paying the mortgage. The tenant should be someone who wants a home like the one you are buying but can't afford it due to cash or credit problems. You enter a lease with an upfront down payment, and then the renter pays the mortgage. Now, this type of deal has two stages. You will lease-to-own, so you pay the rental fee with a small down payment. Once you have the balloon payment at the end, you gain the title to the property. You can choose to rent-to-own for a return of your large investment or keep it as rental property for the long-term investment. In a market, where appreciation is accruing quickly, you may want the quick turnaround of cash, for a new investment versus a long-term rental.

Owner Financing

Owner financing can happen along or in combination with bank financing. It can be a vehicle by which an investor reduces the size of the down payment. In this situation, the owner is willing to finance the purchase of the property, usually by letting the seller take on the default risk of the buyer, as a way to avoid banks. Owner financing gives the seller more income from the interest, and such a property can move quickly in the market. This type of deal works when a buyer is unable to get the full amount from a traditional mortgage required to buy a home. For example, if you have $70,000 to put down on $350,000 and the owner is unwilling to lower the price, but willing to provide financing, you could put the 20% down, make payments, and then in a year or two get a mortgage from a bank. Sometimes the seller will make up only the difference in what you can get from the bank, such as $250,000 from the bank, and needing $380,000, so the seller provides $30,000 to make the deal happen.

Mortgage Assumptions

You take over the mortgage payments for a person, keeping the current terms of the payments intact. The original mortgage holder is released from liability, and you gain it to pay each month. If there is a better rate on the mortgage, than you can obtain from a bank, it makes sense to assume the lease rather than getting a new bank loan on the property. The bank holding the mortgage must agree to your assumption, and sellers need to be current on their loan.

Deferred Maintenance Credits

Deferred maintenance credits are given during closing when the homeowner needs to do repairs but will not. For example, if the mortgage company requires a roof repair, the homeowner may decide to lower the payment of the house in the form of a maintenance credit. The amount provided to the seller would be less the credit, so the buyer can make the correct changes.

Escrow and Reserve Accounts

Escrow is where the money is put on behalf of a real estate sale when a deposit is provided. When an offer is accepted, and to show liquidity, sellers are asked to give a deposit, such as 1% of the purchase price for the house. The money is put into an escrow account until closing and then transferred as part of the full payment to close the deal. Escrow accounts can also be called reserve accounts because the money is reserved to ensure the conditions of the sale are adhered to, including any inspections that must be passed as per the mortgage company's requirements.

Prorated Rent

Prorated rent is one place you might find a cash outlay to make money for a real estate purchase. Prorated rents are designed to cover all days of the month, even when someone moves in days before the first of a new month. For example, if a person is set to move in on March 20, you could charge for the 11 days plus the full month of April. You could also require only the 11 days' worth of rent, plus the security deposit. Most landlords want an entire month, plus a security deposit, and any prorated rent due to ensure they will get their rent.

Security Deposits

Security deposits can give you cash flow and help you buy a new property; however, be careful of using this. Three things can happen. The tenant moves out when their lease is up, and you need to give it back, or you need the money to repair the damages after the tenant leaves. The third is about cash flow and sudden emergency maintenance, where you need to spend the security deposit to make the establishment livable, such as a burst pipe.

Sharing Closing Costs

Closing costs occur in any real estate deal. The number of realtors involved determines the amount of costs and whether there is a mortgage company providing the loan. The buying and seller can share the closing cost. For instance, if the closing cost is $6,000 it can be split so each person pays only $3,000.

Syndicating Deals

Real estate syndication is pooling funds from multiple investors. Funds help you acquire a property, can increase cash flow, and allow you to invest in commercial property. Acquisition fees can give you cash flow if you are the one to find the property, the price is usually 1-5% of the property cost. Asset management fees are another way to gain cash flow through a 1% fee of the gross revenue paid to the manager of the property (you must be the primary caretaker for the property to obtain this fee). Equity participation is compensation for your stake in the project, which could be 5% to 50%, with a rate of return as high as 8% to 12%. The appreciation of the property helps increase the rate of return.

When using the above methods to increase your cash flow and make deals, you do not want to over-burden yourself with too much debt. A wise investor walks away from a deal that will overextend them.

To Have an LLC or Not

An LLC is a limited liability company, which can help you purchase and manage your investments. Real estate investment is a business, and there are tax breaks to be had from registering your rental property as a company. LLCs are one of the best ways to limit your tax liability and gain more deductions. Mortgage companies also like dealing with a business that must carry insurance to operate rather than an individual attempting to get a loan for rental property investment.

Loan Types and Recommendations

A thirty-year fixed mortgage is the best. There are different providers of these long-term mortgages, including Federal Housing Administration (FHA) loans. FHA loans are only available to first-time home buyers and are insured by the government. If you default, the government will cover the mortgage. The banks are also prohibited from charging high fees, but you do need a 3% down payment. An FHA loan can be obtained only once and for up to a four-unit property, only if you move into one of the units.

You want to get your loan through a primary lender to avoid it being sold or from the bank having issues. Some savvy investors go with variable rate loans with a balloon payment, but this is used for fix and flips rather than long-term rental property investments. The Adjustable Rate Mortgage (balloon payment with little down and a variable rate) can become highly expensive if the property does not sell or you do not have the balloon payment after 10 years is up.

What Is PMI?

Private Mortgage Insurance (PMI) is money a bank charges you until you gain 80% equity in the property. The fee covers the financial risk posed by you should you default on the loan and helps reduce the down payment. Federal laws do not stop the bank from requesting the PMI, but they do set the equity limit. When an investor puts 20% down on the property, the bank cannot charge the PMI fee. Some investors have obtained particular loans, where they get 80% from the primary lender and a second loan to cover the 20% down payment, and this prevents the PMI.

FOURTEEN

How to Come Up with the Down Payment

S tarting out, you may not have the down payment readily available in your bank account. There are 15 ways you can get a down payment; note that not all will work based on your current situation.

1. Paying the penalty and removing funds from your 401k early. If you are nowhere near retirement age, taking money out of your retirement account is costly, but it can be made up with the correct investment and put back into the account plus interest, taxes, and fees.

2. HELOC – a home equity line of credit is for people who already own a home and are willing to take out an equity loan to get the down payment for another property.

Be careful you do not overextend the equity and enter a situation where your home is now in negative equity.

3. RELOC – rental equity line of credit, available only if you already have a rental property that you can borrow against the equity.

4. Cross-collateralization – you can put a lien against a home or rental property, then apply for a new loan to buy the rental property. The lien against the property acts as the down payment.

5. Roth IRA – like the 401k option, you can remove money from an IRA or Roth IRA. With a Roth IRA, you have 60 days to pull cash out penalty-free and put it back without incurring tax issues or fees. Roth IRAs can be used to buy your first home, as long as the account is 5 years or older, the funds are used for the purchase, and you are not withdrawing more than $10,000. If all four apply, you will not have to pay fees.

6. House Hacking – a little-used term to mean you have a duplex or multi-family home, and you rent a portion of the home, so the rental payment goes to the mortgage.

7. Seller financing or owner financing can be

one way to get the down payment required to get a traditional loan.

8. Personal loans from friends and family for the down payment are an option.

9. Co-investing, where your family or friends put up the 20% down, is another choice.

10. Selling your stuff may not get enough for the full down payment, but it might make up for the little you are missing.

11. Credit cards are one way you can get cash quickly for a down payment, but it comes with substantial fees, affects your credit score, and your debt to income ratio.

12. Pay off your debts, especially high interest revolving credit like credit cards. Paying off your mortgage frees up monthly income so you can save up for a down payment and then approach a deal when you have collected enough money.

13. Use quantitative methods to help other investors, where you gain an acquisition fee for bringing a property to an investor.

14. Fix and flip a house to raise capital for another property.

15. Refinancing after you renovate your home and take advantage of the new equity.

How Much Money Do I Need for My First House?

This is a loaded question because it depends on how you structure the deal, the down payment, and the selling price. If you do not want to put any money down, then the answer is zero. The above 15 methods include options where you do not provide the down payment, but someone else does.

You also need to account for the realtors and lawyers' fees, which add up to 3 - 4% of the home purchase price. There are title search, insurance, record, and legal fees a buyer pays, and there are costs the seller pays. You can find a deal where the seller pays all the costs to avoid putting any money into the real estate deal.

You can also borrow the down payment, but only if you have qualifying collateral, another bank will let you use to take out equity.

FIFTEEN

Working with the Banks

B anks are a safe and secure way to get funding for your mortgage and first investment property. As an investor, you should work hard to cultivate positive relationships with banks. It is not easy to borrow money after the credit crisis, and a suitable lender is the most valuable business partner to have. Securing a mortgage from a bank can be a very involved process due to the documentation you must supply, the approvals to gain, and the contingencies or conditions the bank may require. You also need to show creditworthiness, with a clear project plan in place to show the debt service coverage, LTV ratio, and find a bank where your plan meets the bank's criteria.

Bank Criteria

Banks require you to meet certain financial qualifications, which includes the following:

- Twenty to 25% down
- A credit score of 740 or higher
- 36% or a lower debt to income ratio

The best deals are found when you meet the above criteria.

You can seek a mortgage broker or banker rather than a significant lender; however, their services come at a price, and not all mortgage brokers are legitimate. Before you take the route of a mortgage broker, assess their fees, the types of loans they are willing to give, and determine if the costs reduce your investment in earning nothing.

I once found a great mortgage broker who said he could get me 6% interest for my loan. However, I was told I needed to do something in the next 60 days to lock in that rate. Mortgage brokers are sharks.

I would say you should not deal with them unless you are unable to get a standard bank loan and if you have exhausted all other options, including family and friends.

Work with a bank and ask for a qualification letter to help estimate the amount they are willing to give you in a loan. A pre-qualification letter provides you with a place to start if you have 20% down. Note, you will verbally provide the specifics, and the letter does not guarantee you that amount. However, you can use the letter to help the seller accept your deal.

If you feel too much pressure to go through with a lending deal or to submit an offer, walk away. Do not buy under pressure. You will only end up getting burned and quite possibly losing all your savings.

Applying for Financing

The core information required to apply through a bank includes:

- Bank application form
- Executive summary
- Current rent details
- Historical financials (2 to 3 years of income, and at least one year of bank statements)
- Copy of leases attached to the property
- Copy of purchase agreement
- Pro forma financials
- Real estate schedule
- Business financials
- State and federal tax returns

Entering your first deal, you are not going to have business documentation; however, the bank will ask for your personal details, copy of the LLC (License of Incorporation), and any funds you have given the company. You need to speak with your bank loan officer to determine what they want based on the deal you are asking about.

The real estate schedule is the one provided by the realtor to tell you when you need certain documents, inspections, and other information submitted, and will include the closing date. This schedule tells you when to have the escrow amount, down payment, and loan money available. The bank needs this to be on time for the deal.

The application begins with a loan officer, who sends it to the underwriters once inspections are conducted. The underwriter provides the loan based on the business plan, amount necessary, down payment, and real estate schedule.

Lender Contingencies

Lenders can require conditions that are met before the closing takes place.

- Appraisal to ensure the home is worth the selling price.
- Environmental reports to ensure nothing harmful is found on the property grounds.

- Property condition assessment, where a third party, such as a contractor, conducts a full assessment.
- Title insurance is required for the loan, where the insurance protects you and the lender against loss should liens, disputes, or other claims be made against the legality of the sale.
- Tenant estoppel certificates are provided if you already have tenants on the property, or they are lined up to move in once the sale is conducted.
- An insurance binder is a document your insurance company will provide the lender to show you have the minimum coverage amounts and are following all covenants of the insurance plan.
- A survey of the property, including property lines, may be required depending on the age of the last one. Older properties may require a more in-depth examination.
- Borrow documents, including resolution and certificate of good standing, may be necessary. These are obtained from your attorney.

Overall, establish a good relationship with a bank and cut down your search options whenever possible.

If one bank denies your loan, chances are all other banks will also say no, until you correct any "high risk" issues, such as low scores, short or inconsistent financial history, or property risk factors (condition of the home).

SIXTEEN

Executing Your First Deal

Y ou have found a property. You want to make an offer, and you have a pre-qualification letter from a bank. What do you do now? Your real estate agent can help you through the process; however, knowing the steps is essential.

#1 Submitting an Offer

There are three ways you can submit an offer.

1. A term sheet is a non-binding expression of your interest in a property, which outlines the price and structure of your transaction. The seller can look at the term sheet and give verbal approval to proceed to the next stage.

2. Letter of Intent is more commonly used by real estate agents, mainly for the more complex transactions, and it is legally binding. In the letter of intent, your agent will want to provide a loophole, such as "based on inspections, surveys," you may or may not be willing to move forward.

3. A purchase agreement is also a legally binding offer, where escrow money, and then the full amount is paid at the end. The purchase agreement still has caveats where the house meets inspection needs according to the bank or buyer.

When you submit an offer, you want to do so with a letter of intent first because it is legally binding and places the house in the "pending sale" category to prevent the seller from accepting other offers before due diligence is finalized.

Once the conditions of the letter intent are satisfied, it is time to enter into a contract. Negotiations and changes to the agreement can still take place.

The contract is where many of the clauses need to outline what will ensure you go through the deal. For example, "the condition of sale is subject to seller qualification with the lender," or the "property must meet clauses as outlined by the lending company."

Contingencies vary based on the home. The older

the house, the more clauses a contract of sale can have.

The most common contingencies are:

1. Appraisal – a request for the property to be appraised by a third party or buyer's bank to ensure the sale price is comparable to the actual house value.
2. Financing – a contingency giving the buyer time to apply and obtain the funding to close on the property.
3. Home sale – the buyer has a specified time to go through the sale of an existing home before they can close on the property with the seller. For example, if you are selling your main property to purchase a rental property you will live in, you may request the new sale is conditional on the sale of your old property.
4. Inspection – due diligence is a must, and banks will require an inspection and the approval report before any other steps are followed. The clause covers you for home repairs the bank requires before they will give you a loan. You can opt out of the purchase or request the purchase price be reduced to cover your repair costs.
5. Sellers have the option of putting in a

kick-out clause, where they can assess
other qualified buyers if you go over your
allotted time to close on the deal.

The contract is a legally enforceable agreement, so you should have as many clauses as protects your purchase rights and investment opportunity. However, be aware that too many terms or contingencies can make the seller wary and not agree to the submitted offer.

#2 Perform Due Diligence

Before you submit an offer and while your offer is being examined, run the numbers. Make sure you understand the potential return on your investment, the NOI, GRM, and the cash flow considerations the deal offers. If a loan or too much down payment is required, where you do not have a positive cash flow, the transaction is not something you want to pursue.

You may decide to pay a due diligence fee, which is a negotiated sum of money, usually $500 to $2,000 (based on the home price) that helps you back out of a deal should something not go right during the inspections and surveys.

- Hire an inspector or contractor.
- Contact your insurance company and other

home insurance companies to assess costs.
Once you choose a company, tell your agent
to start the paperwork on the contingency
the purchase will be completed.

- Get information regarding the utilities,
rents, and other expenses to run the
numbers.

#3 Hire Your Property Manager

You may not want to manage the property if you live remotely from the investment. You need to assess what to evaluate and look for, so you get the right person.

1. Assess the property managers experience
2. Look at the fee structure, such as a fixed amount or percentage, like 8% to 12% of the monthly rent.
3. Does the property manager charge fees when the property is empty? You don't want too many expenses, and most managers do continue to charge whether the property is full, half full, or completely vacant.
4. Determine the tenant screening process, such as complying with the Fair Housing Act.

5. Look at other properties they manage to
   see the average vacancy rate.

By using the checklist above, you can determine if the manager is going to put in as much effort as possible to limit vacancies, or be lazy because they are paid regardless of the place being rented.

#4 Securing Financing

We assessed how to work with banks, but now you need to know what to ask lenders to secure financing. Some useful questions include:

- What are the basic terms of your loans?
- What LTV do you require?
- What is the current interest rate?
- What terms do you offer (30-year fixed)?
- What are the costs?
- Does my loan need a personal guarantee, even though it is under my LLC?
- What size loan are you willing to offer for an LLC investment?
- What are the liquidity and net worth options?
- Do you require a reserve account?
- How long will it take to close on the loan?

The answers help you decide if you want to work

with the mortgage company. You want to make the lender's job easier by having good credit, a low debt to income ratio, and more than the down payment in the bank. You are guaranteed to get approval if your credit scores are in the good to excellent range, you can establish a reserve account of up to a year of mortgage payments, plus the down payment, and your project plan is transparent with all due diligence conducted.

#5 Initiating Closing Process

The closing process will follow the schedule outlined in the purchase agreement; however, if the bank moves faster, you can always request the process end quicker than initially established in the paperwork.

- Set a date for the signing.
- Bring the money or have the bank ready to transfer the funds.
- At the table, the real estate agent will have a stack of paper to sign, they will go over each contingency, each clause, and ask you to sign. Read through the documents to avoid any surprises.
- If you have not, supply your identification, insurance, and any other documentation the real estate asks you to prepare beforehand.

As soon as all the papers are signed, the closing is done. If you entered a deal where you are paid an acquisition fee, you could cash the check. Your closing attorney or agent will handle the paperwork, verify the funds are transferred, and then you get the keys to go to the building.

SEVENTEEN

Give Your New Property a Facelift. Time to Renovate.

D o you know what brings the most value to a home? Home valuations are conducted by bank personnel and tax property professionals; however, they rarely share their list with you for why a property has increased or decreased in value. Before you ever give your property a facelift, decide what you should and should not do. A property that needs to be in livable shape or appeal to a higher-income renter helps you determine the areas to focus on before you invest the money.

We will examine what is worth upgrading and what is worth leaving alone so you can see qualified returns on your rehab expenses. Here are some target points to get you started:

- Who is the average tenant you hope to attract based on the location details?

- You want upgrades that will make an 80% difference in rental rates and overall valuation of the property.
- Only start with 20% of the upgrades you want to make that will ensure an 80% effective rate on valuation.
- Kitchens and bathrooms sell homes, so they are the first places you want to make usable for the renter.
- Always fix things that are broken, including HVAC systems, water heaters, holes in the walls, bathrooms/ showers, and other areas that make the home livable.

Increasing Value

Curb appeal should never be discounted. Think back to a time you rented a home. Perhaps, you were going to college, and you looked at the campus, dorms, and rentals nearby. Was there something about a potential apartment that turned your nose into the air?

People who rent still want a property that looks nice. They want to see the neighborhood to check if your rental is well maintained on the outside because it should equate to a livable functional home inside.

A rented power washer and paint sprayer, and one weekend can ensure the house has more curb appeal. Mowing any lawn space and pulling dead trees and

Amazon USA

Amazon UK

Also, if you have any friends or family who might enjoy this book, spread the love and lend it to them!

Now, I don't just want to sell you a book—I want to see you use what you've learned to build the business of your dreams.

As you work toward your goals, however, you'll probably have questions or may run into some difficulties. I'd like to be able to help you with these! I don't charge for the help, of course, and I answer questions from readers every day.

Here's how we can connect:

Email: Derek@AtmosPublishing.com

Keep in mind I get a lot of emails every day, and answer everything personally, so if you can keep yours as brief as possible, it helps me ensure everyone gets helped!

Thanks again and I wish you the best!

- Derek

bushes will help make the home or rental more appealing.

After you assess the outside, it is time to deal with what is broken or less appealing on the inside.

Bathrooms can deliver up to 70% return on your investment by offering heated flooring, upgraded cabinetry and countertops, and fixtures. The kitchen is the same way. Any stained carpet, areas where there is evidence of a previous leak, or other problems that can affect healthy-living in the home will not only decrease the value but turn away higher-income renters.

Rehabs for Low-Maintenance

Refurbishing a home is also about ensuring you can make it as low-maintenance as possible. If you fear emergency repairs due to the age of an appliance, roof, or another part of the building structure—deal with it immediately. It is far better to replace carpet and other flooring, appliances, and the roof before renters move in versus losing the renter because they are unhappy with the ill-repair of the home or your much-needed attention each week.

Efficiency Upgrades

A fine line exists between upgrading a home for more efficiency and leaving it be, and it comes down to getting a higher-income renter and your ROI. Will spending $3,000 on new windows be enough to make a home more efficient?

An example is a 1920s home with single-pane windows. The area around the windows leak, new weatherstripping is necessary, and every time the wind blows dirt comes in the house around the window. Imagine the amount of heat loss. A renter is going to look at the problem and see dollar signs going up on their heating bill. Saving the renter ensures you have a long-term tenant, and you get the costs back in the rent you charge.

Installing new windows and motion-sensing light switches when you are paying the utilities is imperative. Cut your costs as much as possible with the upgrades so that you can have a positive cash flow and high ROI. If you pay water, sewer, and garbage, install a water meter that limits water usage to specific gallons.

Some people would recommend making a property bigger or smarter, with smart fridges and other gadgets. Thermostats and motion-sensing lights are the only "smart" devices you want to offer in a medium-income location because it helps cut down on electricity usage, particularly if you pay the costs.

As for going bigger, on a rental, the costs usually outweigh the return on the investment. Don't add on, unless it is the only way you can get another apartment or room rented.

Estimating the Rehab

If you have no experience in fixing and flipping, construction, or similar service industry, get at least three estimates from professionals per type of job. A plumber should offer an estimate of any plumbing issues like a leaky faucet. A contractor should look at the cosmetic and structural changes, including a kitchen and bathroom redo, versus an electrician that would examine the costs for new fixtures or upgraded wiring.

Each state has material costs, and they can differ significantly, so it is unwise to tell you the exact way to estimate the expenses a rehab might be. The best option is to speak with a professional, even if you go into a furniture store and ask for the cheapest cabinets for a kitchen redesign to see the costs associated with just the materials.

Hiring professionals when you have no experience is imperative to ensure you are not missing structural issues or underestimating the trouble the rehab can cause. If you ever watch HGTV where someone buys a fix and flip and realizes their budget is maxed out due to a structural issue, you know what this can mean for upgrading your rental beyond just livable.

Getting Started

The magnitude of your goals can be overwhelming. The key to achieving your goals are to break them down into manageable chunks so you can keep the correct mindset for your rental property investment. Taking the first step is always the hardest part of starting your business, and it will set you apart as one of the successful investors. The information and your first step apply whether you are buying your first property or trying to set up a deal that you have no experience with.

Commit to taking one step each day, where you ensure you follow a consistent plan to meet your success. If you can do this, you will look back at your hesitation and worry, and see the amazing progress you have made.

Phone Conversations

Here is one way you can take your first step—make a phone call—speak with a realtor.

> Hi, I am___, I am looking for a long-term partnership for my real estate investment business and saw your qualifications online. I am looking to invest in properties with a price between $200,000 and $400,000, multi-unit homes, or apartments. May I set up an appointment to discuss my business outline?

You want to continue looking over the information in this book while taking your first steps. The way to make this happen is by establishing your network. You can talk to every real estate agency in your investment area until you find the one person who will be a good fit.

Next, where are you getting your down payment on the first property? Do you have it, or do you need investors?

Here is an opening pitch for a landlord association:

> I enjoyed listening to your talk tonight. I want to start in rental property investment, but I want to do it right, and you sound like the

person who would be a perfect mentor if you have the time?

Cold-Emails

Like cold calling, you can also structure some emails to get attention.

Your email should begin with flattery based on facts without using superlatives. Mention a blog, newsletter, book, review, success story, or other information you learned about the person you want to approach and add to your network.

In 2 to 3 sentences, state your goals and how they can help.

End the query, with a call to action, requesting they return your email with some resources or confirmation they would be willing to meet you and help you one-on-one.

You can take these email or phone call steps each day, as you read, and look for a property to invest in, so you feel as if you are making your way to your larger goal.

Afterword

A foundation is essential to success in rental property investments. You know your mindset is imperative to follow-through and make your first property purchase. Long-term success is only gained when you have the necessary skills, stable goals, and a network to make up for the knowledge you lack.

Once the process becomes a routine, it is a matter of taking the investment strategies and steps covered in this book to help you begin.

Owning rental property is not without its disadvantages, including pipes breaking, minor and major repairs, and problem tenants. However, from the discussion of market analysis and passive income successes, you know with the correct foundation, knowledge, and mindset, you can make additional income each month, and retire early.

Your success is based on your goals, action, and

expecting real, measurable results. We overviewed how to get started with a step by step look at rental property investment deals and the downfalls others have made, such as not understanding a good deal and closing on a property. We made sure you had references to look back on regarding property classes and types to help you make a successful deal based on your starting capital or lack thereof.

I delivered on location research resources, how to choose a property, including what makes the best rental investment compared to other properties on the market.

Combining the formulas with analyzing deals for the best opportunities, you know how to assess the gross scheduled income, expenses, and recalculate the deal for fair market value.

Not only do you have the tools, but you also have websites and resources throughout this book that ensure you can find your first deal and many others from now on and happily sit back while rental income comes in.

There is nothing more daunting than the purchase methods and knowing you need a down payment unless someone is willing to back you with an investment. You learned finding an investor or partner can lead to zero down payments from you, although it does reduce the profit you make.

Working with banks is time-consuming but rewarding. You now have the step by step process for what a bank will ask you to do before signing the contract to your new rental property.

You cannot forget the pitfalls of working with mortgage brokers, plus going with an investor relationship that may turn against you. You were shown why you want to execute your first deal with your eyes wide open, using a bank and real estate professional to submit the agreement, negotiate the contract, and handle the closing.

Discussing some motivational tips to get started, you also gained a few opening lines to approach people you want in your network, including how to structure a cold email. These small scripts can always be improved on, so you gain the right deal with the right team.

The two last things I will ask of you is to clearly think about the one thing you learned from this book to help you make the deal. I hope it was that your mindset must be firm on beginning a rental property investment business before you even purchase property, so that you can be successful.

Would You Do Me A Favor?

Thank you for buying my book. I'm positive that if you just follow what I've written, you will be on your way to building a profitable freedom business.

I have a tiny favor to ask. Would you mind taking a minute to write a blurb on Amazon about this book? I check all my reviews and love to get feedback (that's the real reward for my work—knowing that I'm helping people).

Go to either of these 2 links to leave an Amazon review:

Amazon USA: https://amzn.to/2Aq3oA1

Amazon UK: https://amzn.to/2Ayzvhj

Or use the QR codes on the next page:

Resources

Academy, P. M. (2019). 10 Qualities - Be a Successful Property Investor. Retrieved from http://www.propertymasteryacademy.co.uk/news/10-qualities-to-make-you-a-successful-property-investor/

Buczynski, B. (2018, June 4). 5 Proven Ways to Increase Home Value. Retrieved from https://www.nerdwallet.com/blog/mortgages/how-to-increase-home-value/

Camargo, M. (2019, August 9). FICO® scores vs. credit scores: What's the difference? Retrieved from https://www.creditkarma.com/credit-cards/i/fico-score-vs-credit-score/

Carson, C. (2019, November 17). How to Run the Numbers For Rental Properties – Back-of-the-Envelope Analysis. Retrieved from https://www.coachcarson.com/run-the-numbers-investment-properties/

Christopher, N. (2018, November 14). Is It Time To Hire A Property Manager For Your Single-Family Rental Investments? Retrieved from https://www.forbes.com/sites/forbesrealestatecouncil/2018/11/14/is-it-time-to-hire-a-property-manager-for-your-single-family-rental-investments/#9e6f2a36f4de

Davis, B. G. (2019, November 1). 15 Clever Ways to Come Up with a Down Payment for a Rental Property | SparkRental. Retrieved from https://sparkrental.com/15-clever-ways-down-payment-for-rental-property/

December 5, J. 2. S. A. 2. A. (2019, November 26). Top 18 Biggest Mistakes When Buying Rental Property. Retrieved from https://www.realwealthnetwork.com/learn/top-18-biggest-mistakes-when-buying-rental-property/

Diaries, C. F. (2016, May 25). Is Your Mindset the Key to Rental Property Investing Success? Retrieved from http://www.cashflowdiaries.com/mindset-needed-to-rental-property-success/

Foy, N. (2019, June 11). Real Estate Due Diligence Checklist for Buying Investment Property. Retrieved from https://www.under30wealth.com/property-under-contract-checklist-what-to-do-next/

Fragale, B. J. (2020, February 10). What's the Best Type of Commercial Real Estate Property for Investors? Retrieved from https://www.biggerpockets.com/blog/2015-08-31-top-10-questions-commercial-mortgage-broker

Investopedia. (2019, August 29). Contingency Clauses in Home Purchase Contracts. Retrieved from https://www.investopedia.com/articles/personal-finance/102913/contingency-clauses-home-purchase-contracts.asp

Group, F. (2019). Term Sheet vs. Letter of Intent vs. Purchase Agreement | The FBB Group, Ltd. Retrieved from https://www.fbb.com/company-information/recentarticles/term-sheet-vs-letter-of-intent-vs-purchase-agreement

Investopedia. (2019, October 1). How to Calculate the ROI on a Rental Property. Retrieved from https://www.investopedia.com/articles/investing/062215/how-calculate-roi-rental-property.asp

Investopedia. (2019, October 13). Capitalization Rate Definition. Retrieved from https://www.investopedia.com/terms/c/capitalizationrate.asp

Investopedia. (2019). Escrow. Retrieved from https://www.investopedia.com/terms/e/escrow.asp.

Investopedia. (2019, July 22). How Cash-on-Cash Returns Work. Retrieved from https://www.investopedia.com/terms/c/cashoncashreturn.asp

Manolas, K. (2019, December 16). Should You Create an LLC For Your Rental Property? Retrieved from https://www.avail.co/education/articles/should-you-create-an-llc-for-your-rental-property

Quickenloans. (2019). What Is Mortgage Assumption and Why Might You Do It. Retrieved from https://

www.quickenloans.com/learn/what-is-mortgage-assumption-and-why-might-you-do-it.

Raybould, H. (2019, September 3). How To Develop The Right Mindset For Property Investment. Retrieved from https://creativepg.com/how-to-develop-the-right-mindset-for-property-investment/

Real Estate Express. (2019, March 11). 12 Real Estate Professionals Share Their Budgeting Tips. Retrieved from https://www.realestateexpress.com/career-hub/grow-your-real-estate-career/real-estate-budgeting-tips/

Stillman, J. (2020, February 6). 5 Steps to Get the Right Mindset for Success. Retrieved from https://www.inc.com/jessica-stillman/5-steps-to-get-the-right-mindset-for-success.html